Praise for *Limitless*

A powerfully profound book to tap into your intuition, visualization skill set, self-healing, and unleash the free flow of creativity.

Emma Mildon
Bestselling author of *The Soul Searcher's Handbook*
and *Evolution of Goddess*.

In this book, Ms. Flack hands readers the keys to unlock old prison doors and free themselves from patterns they might believe are permanent parts of their lives. If you long to gain clarity and gently release struggles from your experience, this book can help. Did you know that what the author describes as "bookmarked pictures in your mind" are thought structures that manifest as physical grooves called neural pathways? This means that you can carve new neural pathways that allow for experiences that you might believe are impossible for you. This book teaches you to tune deeply into your intuition; use research-based practices drawn from neuroscience, psychology, and trauma-recovery work; and rewrite the story of your life. Read this book if you are ready to experience the full life you were meant to live.

Jacob Nordby
author of *The Creative Cure–How Finding and Freeing Your Inner Artist Can Heal Your Life*

Limitless by Gwyneth Flack is an invitation to rediscover your true self—a profound journey of remembering who you are at your core. Through compelling personal stories, insightful guidance, and practical exercises, Gwyneth gently leads you toward alignment of mind, body, and soul, helping you fully embrace your creative self-expression and life's purpose. Each chapter concludes with key takeaways and simple, actionable activities, offering continued support as you deepen your connection with intuition and your highest self.

Anita Adams
Bestselling author of *Whispers of the Soul*

Gwyneth Flack was a sensitive, star-gazing child who experienced an NDE (near death experience) at only four years old. (She also had a pet racoon as a kid—how fun is that?!) Deeply connected and incredibly wise, in these pages, she teaches us to say "Hello" to our inner knowing, our physical bodies, and our soul presence. If you want to cultivate your intuitive gifts, you will love the practical teachings, personal anecdotes and easy to implement exercises in each chapter. She shares real life examples of when intuition saved her life and reminds us that increasing our intuitive awareness helps us to feel more grounded, increases our connection with others and helps us to heal old patterns so we can more easily access our creativity.

Elizabeth Barbour
author of *Sacred Celebrations: Designing Rituals to Navigate Life's Milestone Transitions*

I love this book! I think it's absolutely fantastic. I haven't ever seen or heard of a book specifically addressing what is one of the greatest hurdles most people who wish to develop their intuitive awareness and abilities who are also intellectually capable have to get over. This book helps people to take the "leap of faith" beyond their intellects in order to gain certainty in Spirit and have their intuitive and higher creative abilities all working together. The time is here for many souls to experience that transformation, and I'm delighted Gwyneth wrote this book.

Michael J. Tamura,
internationally renowned spiritual teacher and author of
You Are the Answer: An Extraordinary Guide to Entering the Sacred Dance with Life and Fulfilling Your Soul Purpose

LIMITLESS

TRANSFORM YOUR LIFE
WITH INTUITION AND CREATIVITY

GWYNETH FLACK

Copyright © 2025 by Gwyneth Flack

Limitless
Transform Your Life with Intuition and Creativity

All rights reserved.
No part of this work may be used or reproduced, transmitted, stored, or used in any form or by any means graphic, electronic, or mechanical, including but not limited to photocopying, recording, scanning, digitizing, taping, Web distribution, information networks or information storage and retrieval systems, or in any manner whatsoever without prior written permission from the publisher.

In this world of digital information and rapidly-changing technology, some citations do not provide exact page numbers or credit the original source. We regret any errors, which are a result of the ease with which we consume information.

Without in any way limiting the author's and publisher's exclusive rights under copyright, any use of this publication to train generative artificial intelligence (AI) or Large Language Model (LLM) technologies to generate text is expressly prohibited.

Senior Editor: Laurie Knight
Developmental Editor: Amy Delcambre
Cover Designer: Kristina Edstrom

An Imprint for GracePoint Publishing (www.GracePointPublishing.com)

GracePoint Matrix, LLC
624 S. Cascade Ave, Suite 201, Colorado Springs, CO 80903
www.GracePointMatrix.com Email: Admin@GracePointMatrix.com
SAN # 991-6032

A Library of Congress Control Number has been requested and is pending.

ISBNs: 978-1-961347-88-5
eISBN: 978-1-961347-78-6
Audio ISBN: 978-1-966346-01-2

Books may be purchased for educational, business, or sales promotional use.
For distribution queries contact Sales@IPGBbook.com
For non-retail bulk order requests contact Orders@GracePointPublishing.com

Printed in U.S.A

Contents

DEDICATION III

INTRODUCTION V

CHAPTER ONE: REMEMBER HOW POWERFUL YOU ARE 1
    INTUITIVE TOOLS 12

CHAPTER TWO: BOOKMARKED PICTURES IN YOUR MIND 17
    INTUITIVE TOOLS 35

CHAPTER THREE: MANAGE YOUR INTELLECT AND OVER-THINKING MIND TO HAVE MORE FUN AND GET MORE DONE 41
    INTUITIVE TOOLS 53

CHAPTER FOUR: GROUNDING: A PRESENT AND HEALING RELATIONSHIP WITH YOUR BODY 59
    INTUITIVE TOOLS 73

CHAPTER FIVE: BUILDING EVERYDAY TRUST WITH YOUR AMAZING INTUITION 78
    INTUITIVE TOOLS 103

CHAPTER SIX: LAUGH YOUR WAY TO EASIER COMMUNICATION AND LIFE NAVIGATION 107
    INTUITIVE TOOLS 127

CHAPTER SEVEN: BE THE CONSCIOUS CREATIVE DIRECTOR OF YOUR LIFE 137
    INTUITIVE TOOLS 158

ACKNOWLEDGEMENTS 167

ABOUT THE AUTHOR 169

Dedication

To the late Michael J. Tamura, an extraordinary teacher and friend. Your generosity of spirit, teaching, and laughter lives on!

Introduction

Within the space of one busy day, you're faced with a variety of decisions, each with their own valuable pathway into the world. You may spend weeks trying to make a key decision. *Hello* intuition!

If you were paying attention to your intuition, you knew the answer the first moment you asked yourself the question of what to do. In this world, it's very easy to turn down your inner knowing or allow something louder to drown it out. When decisions are made from your intuitive awareness, you save time and energy because your direction is allied with your purpose, integrity, life skills, creativity, and self-knowledge. This inner teamwork brings incredible outer results!

Our cultural pattern of overthinking without a pause for inner guidance has left us missing the language for accessing our inner knowledge and creative power. Overthinking crowds the mind and blocks the space within the self that allows for deeper healing of past experiences which would result in positive growth. Without making intuitive awareness a conscious practice, it is easy to unconsciously absorb emotions, opinions, or directives from your daily environment. This impacts the way you feel, think, make choices, and relate with others. Think of the gut microbiome. Evidence reveals that the gut's biome impacts all health. Not unlike how ultra processed foods or chemical additives negatively impact the gut's natural biome, consider how everything impacts and interrupts clear seeing and intuition. When we clean up our personal, spiritual biome we allow inner health that restores to balance the innate expression of our wholeness. Healing happens effortlessly when we experience the spaciousness of our intuitive awareness at work in everyday life, consciously.

Remarkably, brilliant ideas are born from your intuitive knowing. You apply your intellect (learned knowledge) to fine tune or edit them. Consciously cultivating this teamwork streamlines and elevates it to higher levels. Never forget that you are the creative director of your life. Your awareness is your all-access, backstage pass to know yourself and consciously update to your latest operating system. Imagination is a springboard for deepening intuition, healing, and creative power.

These are just a few reasons why living intuitively brings me joy and laughter and expands my vision of the world. From a set of narrow corridors to an open space of amazing alliances and insights, I explore and discover the world and myself. I love this kind of exploration, and I imagine that you may, too.

Wherever I go and whatever I do, I'm simultaneously a teacher and student as I learn something new that I can also teach. Though society directs our attention to dramatic events that teach or inspire people, I learn equally from observing the less obvious, subtle, overlooked events or interactions around me and in the larger world. Why? Because seemingly small, inner-lead choices clear our runway for take-off and landing versus us plowing full-speed ahead and banging into every obstacle in our paths. I have certainly tried the full-speed method; perhaps you have too. When you forget to pause and observe, it's like you are wearing blinders.

Most people grow up in a nonintuitive culture, where from a young age society encourages us to ignore inner knowing when considering the best route to choose. Instead, we are expected to blast through obstacles to achieve goals. The debris left from nonintuitive strategies usually shows up as stress, anxiety, conflict, confusion, subtle fears, or burnout.

As a teacher and writer, I use the words *intuitive, intuitive awareness, inner knowing, inner guidance, intuitive knowing, clear seeing,* and *clairvoyance* to reference the innate experiences and abilities that everyone has. Some people are surprised to hear that I have taught many two-year clairvoyance courses to mental health professionals, nurses, doctors, professors, schoolteachers, business entrepreneurs, acupuncturists, artists, writers, parents, and others.

Many people associate the word *clairvoyance* differently from what it is. Keep in mind that this is just another word to describe innate abilities that have limitless beneficial applications when integrated with our gifts, learned skills, and life experiences. The people who most often seek my teaching and private sessions are people helping others in the world in a myriad of ways, both recognized and unrecognized. This kind of growth nourishes, supports, expands, and replenishes their inner well, and allows them to clearly distinguish their own true energy from what they have absorbed from the world around them. Once you consciously say *Hello* to your inner abilities, you can easily develop and integrate them into your daily life for greater awareness, joy, and enhanced creativity.

Teaching was actually the farthest thing from my mind at the time I began attending meditation classes on healing, spiritual growth, and clairvoyance with my husband. My goal at that time was to create a balanced life that included building a house and an organic maple syrup business, writing, and becoming a parent. The inner growth and awareness I experienced was a joyful work in progress, improving all the conditions of my inner and outer existence. I'd always known that I was good at communicating with, helping, and understanding people; I just didn't yet realize I had something to share as a teacher.

This work was also to create a dynamic foundation for a long-term partnership with my husband. Intuitively, we learned to give each other enough space to keep growing our relationship toward greater light or awareness. Intuitive awareness helps us find neutrality, creativity, and humor for stronger communication and effective solutions not only in our marriage—and as parents—but also in our other relationships.

This expansion of awareness was profoundly valuable and freeing. It validated the multitudes of intuitive experiences I had had since I was a small child, including a near-death experience (NDE). My parents, trained as PhD scientists, taught me to observe the natural world as interrelated, rather than as a bunch of separate parts. I became able to apply those observational skills on an intuitive level in relation to people, communication, healing, and creative power.

As I integrated my inner growth and expressed it in the world around me in many different settings, people began to get curious about my insights. I encouraged them to take some classes like I was doing, getting on a plane four times a year to gather with people from all walks of life for a weekend of extraordinary growth and healing.

I became a teacher when people started asking me, "How about you teach us?" I happily accepted the challenge as I had been an enthusiastic, lifelong adventurer, engaging in such things as building a house and business, traveling, taking wilderness trips, moving to the United States as a child where I lived in a tent for eight months until my parents built a house, or exploring my own mind to discover, grow, and heal. After teaching my first six-week class, I was invited to teach series after series. Eventually, I cofounded a center, which served the New England area and Canada for ten years.

Why I Wrote This Book and What to Expect

When I teach, there's always so much more that I'd like to share in each class if there was more time, such as teaching stories, in-depth descriptions of the intuitive, creative, overthinking mind, and new ways of relating with the world. In addition to my own experiences and personal knowledge, this book is inspired by thousands of private sessions and classes that I've given during the past seventeen years and by stories from my students (details changed to protect their privacy) which I use to highlight topics throughout this book.

This book has been delightful to write, while also a challenge in finding words that convey the experiences, insights, and aha moments of my students, myself, and others. If you are a busy, dynamic, intuitive person who wants to learn how your intellect and creativity can collaborate as a team by discovering overlooked aspects of yourself, this book is for you.

Introduction

At the end of each chapter, you will find tools and activities related to the chapter theme. Each activity is grounded in creative visualization, a successful method used by Olympic athletes, therapists, and coaches, and something I've taught for seventeen years. As the activities build upon each other, by the end of this book, you will have a navigational toolkit equipping you with intuitive practices that you can apply on the go anytime or anywhere. As you read this book, my hope is you realize you have abilities and skills you can bring to light in new ways! Get ready to experience clearer decision-making, personal healing, and limitless creativity.

Chapter One
Remember How Powerful You Are

Remember and Recognize Your Intuition

Like a houseplant near a window, you are hardwired to reach toward the bright light of your conscious awareness and inner knowing. You might not always remember where this place of infinite wholeness is located. Sometimes, you can feel like a boat lost in the ocean. Without navigational tools, finding the way back can be tricky.

This disconnection from your intuitive awareness can cause stress, loneliness, worry, anger, self-worth issues, self-doubt, fear, guilt, or grief. When feeling these emotions, ask the deeper question: *Have I forgotten my intuition in this moment?* Your intuition is your navigational tool.

When you steer a course from your inner knowing, you create space to be spiritually graceful, purposefully creative, and emotionally playful. You become more adept at handling the extreme landscapes of human existence.

Within us lies a remembering that is familiar, yet often out of reach because inner guidance is not validated in our society. For instance, have you ever known something, but didn't fully believe it until you later had actual proof it was true? This is partly due to the way the nervous system automatically interprets everything it encounters. Your intellect takes your life experiences and creates an imprint of image data, a template. Like an outdated operating system, these templates come from past patterning, rather than what is unfolding in the present. The result?

> ***You don't see what you don't know or know what you don't see.***

Spiritual growth happens when you allow an internal update to your data templates. This is commonly known as healing. When you allow an update, you optimize your life and restore harmony and collaboration within your intuitive biome.

Your nervous system and brain are housed in your body, yet you are more than just a body and intellect. Imagine yourself as the wise and loving guardian for the divine temple of expression called your body. Your body has incredible senses: touch, sight, hearing, smell, and taste. Intuitive awareness becomes a harmonizing bridge to your body. Since some of your past experiences might not support your current goals, more intuitive awareness can gently encourage your body to come on board and achieve those goals.

Many Olympic athletes use creative visualization to reset their patterning, rewire their nervous systems, and achieve their goals, while therapists and coaches use it to help their clients envision a new way forward. Whether a person consciously recognizes it or not, this is a way to step outside of old data templates and allow a refresh. In their imagination, they might see, or simply know, the clearest path forward. An athlete might imagine how they'll pace themselves, navigate, or correct a multitude of unpredictable situations, such as external factors like weather or inner negative feedback.

This moves them out of a thinking-dominant state of wanting, where they desire to make this happen but a part of them has doubts. This is a way that anyone can harmonize with their body and say, "*Hello* Body. We are having a powerful new experience now." Inner permission (allowing) fuels the imagination to stretch beyond limits.

> *Inner permission is totally free, and it creates real change.*

Your inner knowing can help you improve in areas that may seem stuck, where you can access better choices as you need them and create something new rather than recycle the past. This process starts in your imagination, which can rewire your nervous system and reset your physical response. This sets up an opportunity for a redo in any area that's ripe for change, such as emotional blocks, mental blocks, fear, anxiety, or speaking your truth. It can produce change in how you communicate, organize your life, spiritual growth, trusting yourself, healing from trauma, or experiencing greater love and compassion. You become conscious about what you are imagining.

Origins of Intuitive Awareness

You come to the planet as an imaginative, bright, creative, curious being, with a full spectrum of love, receptivity, laughter, personal power, and undivided awareness. For a short time, you are one with your infinite wholeness. This awareness is different from your intellect. At this tender age, you are not capable of thinking about separation, compartmentalization, polarization, or self-criticism. Hold a newborn baby for a few quiet moments, and you'll feel the peace of pure presence. This can feel like deep stillness.

Your first year on planet earth, you slowly forget this awareness. You focus on your unique body with its delights and limitations. You also become intent on experiencing your environment.

By the time you turn two, you experience *two*. Two means the dual nature of relationships. Creativity originates in oneness and is expressed in duality. It's easy to forget that all relationships originate from one primary relationship—with yourself. Society encourages you to self-determine from intellect and analysis instead of going into your inner knowing. Without validation of all you truly are, you eventually forget your foundational relationship with your inner guidance.

Remembering the Movement of Creation

In your heart, you long to grow through the intuitive creation that courses through your mind, body, and senses in a powerful, purposeful flow. The world around you is linear and intellectual, but your creative rhythm has no logic or methodology.

> *Creation always begins in the imagination with no hierarchy, rules, top, bottom, or sides.*

Begin anywhere. Creativity is totally inclusive. Your imagination is your springboard, your intuitive biome. You can navigate intuitively within any area of your life. You have free will to ignore it, but your inner knowing quietly remains. Like a house with many rooms, you can switch off the lights, but the room is still there when you're ready to return.

When you experience the movement of creation, you remember your infinite essence. This flow might surface when you're immersed in nature, or maybe through a poem, or an idea, or insight that appears out of nowhere. Sometimes, it appears when you spontaneously speak from your heart or hear with clarity. Perhaps you suddenly envision a valuable next step, or you have an inspiration while creating music or skiing down a mountain in a rhythmic flow that goes beyond mechanical thinking.

This powerful, sacred flow brings with it a sense of effortless freedom. Most people have tapped into the current of intuitive creation but afterward they can't name what happened. Bringing consciousness to it empowers you to be the creative director of your life and brings orchestration into more areas, especially where you might be stuck.

Intuition, Interconnection, and Communication

Everything is connected to everything else. Each moment is an opportunity to experience those interrelations and to access the compassion, receptivity, and power of your inner knowing.

The earth gives us a beautiful example of interconnected wisdom. In the soil lives a mind-boggling network of mycelia, tiny fungi filaments that form a communication network and play an essential role in ecosystems by regenerating soil and delivering nutrients. Trees access the network to communicate with other trees. Mycelia is a representation of our own interwoven relationships and how humans affect one another. Trees need communication, and so do we.

Imagine if you had an inseparable, deep relationship, but you never acknowledged it. The relationship would slowly erode. You might even doubt the relationship ever existed. Eventually, communication lines between you would disappear.

A Thinking-Dominant Culture

Intuition is the mycelia of your personal ecosystem, interwoven with your intellect, senses, and other systems. Your intellect is essential. However, a thinking-dominant culture focuses solely on intellect and critical analysis for problem-solving. It has no language for accessing intuitive knowledge. Without a language, you have no permission to trust your inner knowing. As a result, the collective favors intellect over intuition and remains mostly unconscious.

> *Your intuition is direct and honest, yet it makes no demands.*

Intuition brings up creative solutions beyond the ability of your thinking mind. Inside you is the gift of orchestrated creation. However, without your conscious guidance, your intellect will often demand concrete physical evidence in a misdirected context. This imbalance can cause you to doubt your inner guidance, ideas, voice, or true feelings. From a young age, you were trained to intellectually defend or prove what you know or believe. In the correct context, this is valuable. Yet, this often overflows into other areas of your life where a different approach is more effective.

Subtle cues from others can have a negative impact on how you feel, such as trusting your ideas, making decisions, speaking your truth, or healing outdated patterns. Your intellect easily goes into a type of survival thinking which shows up as overthinking and negative self-talk. Perfectionism or comparison is a good example of this, where you try to match the energy of the nonstop world around you, to your own detriment.

Imagine you are seven years old, and you receive a valuable insight from your inner knowing that contains the seeds of a gift you will share with others when you're older. When you share it, you get no response from the adults around you, or maybe they rebuke you. In both cases, they feel responsible to tell you how *they* see the world.

You can't prove your intuitive observation with physical evidence, because first of all, you're seven! Plus, you can't find the words to describe your awareness in intellectual terms, so it's like you're speaking a language they've lost the ability to hear. As a result, you wonder if what you shared has any significance at all. This experience undermines your intuitive ability to recognize what holds value for you—especially, that you have unquantifiable worth.

> *Inner knowing is not trying to survive, so it has nothing to defend.*

On the other hand, the intellect can create a lot of stress following an intuitive download. The intellect wants to define what just happened. In this situation, you are like someone who has just gone through a life-changing occurrence, and someone else tries to tell *you* what happened to you. You feel invalidated. Ever have that happen to you as an adult (or child)?

Because of this setup, sometimes you might merge into your intellect and forget you are also intuitive. In a world where inner guidance is not assigned value, you can easily lose sight of your innermost wisdom.

As a culture, we are becoming more and more aware of networks on every imaginable level: between mycelia and trees, humans and climate change, soil and water health and life, and between the neural networks within our central nervous system. These systems have always been there, but we have not always seen or been aware of them. In the same way, our intuitive awareness is largely invisible in our society. Sometimes, what is hardest to see is actually right in front of us! It's our personal ecosystem and it's not separate from the whole of life.

By balancing intuition with intellect, you can positively impact relationships on global scales. Being intuitive isn't about living in a bubble where you have all the answers and don't need anything from anyone. It's about consciously recognizing the myriad ways you are supported throughout the global web of life where you collaboratively grow and create with others.

When you live in conscious awareness and in tune with your inner guidance, you have clarity to set the quality of your day, whether you have a challenging week or you're on vacation. Small intuitive choices allow you to access an abundant flow of support in your daily life. Living this way enhances your joy and laughter, too.

You are more than a brain and nervous system with quantifiable outcomes. Not everything is known, identified, or named. You have unquantifiable value. Your deepest wisdom and brightest awareness could be referred to as *soul*, without any religious context. Some use the words *presence*, *spirit*, *higher self*, or *light*. There are many words, and yet no words, to describe that we are all unique expressions of infinite oneness.

> ***Your body and soul are a creative team.***

Anyone can have this collaboration in their everyday lives to support them every step of the way. Your presence expresses wisdom through your body in powerful, creative, intuitive ways.

Gwyneth Flack

My Intuitive Origin Story

When I was three years old, my mother took me to play school for the first time. When we arrived at the gate leading into the schoolyard, I told my mother, "No, I don't need you to come in with me, I can do it myself!" My mother laughingly remembers this moment.

I was genuinely embarrassed to have her drop me off at school. In my mind, I was too old to be accompanied, because I didn't feel like a toddler. Inside, I was already a teenager. I was aware that I was a soul presence, not just a body.

I was so adamant about my independence that my mother had to agree to stay behind. Reasoning didn't work for me. She hid behind a hedge, watching to be sure I arrived safely with my teacher. I felt like an old soul trapped in a little person's body. Didn't anybody see me? *Hello*? I wondered if perhaps I really was only three. Maybe the cosmic joke was on me. Was this all there was, or was there something more to this experience called life?

I received a clear answer to my question a year later, when I was four. I was walking barefoot in the garden and stepped on a bee that stung me. Immediately, my body went into anaphylactic shock. My mother quickly put me in the car and raced toward the tiny hospital in our New Zealand village. I sat next to my sister, feeling profoundly sleepy during the car ride. I had trouble breathing and faded in and out of consciousness. My sister said I was turning blue. At the hospital, right in time, an injection of adrenaline brought me back.

I clearly recall lying on the table in the hospital while simultaneously looking at my body from above. I was completely aware of being a bright soul presence. From the ceiling I observed, *My body is down there, but here I am. I'm fine. I'm still here, and my body is there.* What a difference! I wasn't having any trouble breathing, yet my body was! Without the life I brought to my body, it would cease to be.

These observations were powerful. I was more than my four-year-old physical form. In that moment, I was saying *Hello* to the brighter me! I was free. I could choose to stay or go. I saw everything happening in the room through peaceful observation without judgment or fear. Time was neither fast nor slow.

> *I experienced only awareness, unconnected to an age or even a body. This awareness did not come from intellectual language, so I couldn't fully explain it.*

After I arrived back in my body, I tuned in to the people around me who were thrilled that I was okay. I was a bit shocked, but the out-of-body experience was, in some ways, unremarkable to me. Because it was beyond language and I was four, after describing what happened, I had little more to say about it. Since this awareness was an innate state of being, my mind asked, *Doesn't everyone have daily access to this awareness? Doesn't everyone know this state of beingness?*

After a night in the hospital, I went home with this crystalline awareness. I was not merely physical anatomy and an intellect. *I brought life to my body.* Words could hardly express what a relief this was to me, because I'd never felt like I was just a kid. Society saw me as only four, which made me feel unseen, reduced into a compartment, an object with not enough space to be. I also felt disconnected, alone in the world.

> *Looking at the stars had been my way to remember that I was part of something beyond one physical body, on one single planet. I realized that feeling alone comes from forgetting all that I am as a bright presence.*

This experience was beyond my intellect. Intellect could not quantify my awareness; it could only invalidate it. Luckily, even at four my imagination was a healthy habitat where I envisioned beyond any bounds. My brush with death was a celebration, because it validated the infinite. It was a *Hello* to living from conscious awareness! My near-death experience was a lifetime commitment ceremony, highlighting my joyful and powerful soul presence, an invitation for me to stay on my awareness path, while helping others to see the brighter and bigger aspects of who they are.

You are a powerful creator. Your brightest answers come through the distillation of your experiences in collaboration with your intuitive knowing. At some particular junction, you are nudged toward looking within, to remember who you are in a way that will be unforgettable. At first, this gift may appear like a loss, failure, accident, or illness. You might spot the gift immediately, or you might need some adjustment before you see it for what it is and transform your experiences into wisdom, inner trust, and inner knowing. This is how you update to the most current version of your operating system.

When I was in elementary school, my mother took me to her office party. I went over to her colleague and said, "You are very different on the inside than you are on the outside." He was bemused and slightly intrigued. He knew I was on to something, yet he wasn't entirely sure how to respond because he was trained to look outside, not inside.

We were both intuitive, yet he didn't think of himself that way. This man was a highly capable professional who read people before hiring them and could discern if someone was lying. I offered him this intuitive reading to help evolve his soul path and make his life more streamlined and joyful. I gave it from the energy of honesty and love. I saw in him a sensitive, kind person wearing a thick veneer that blocked his access to his inner guidance.

I saw that long ago he'd been reduced into a compartmentalized construct. He had forgotten his soul presence and his pure creative power. In less than a second, all this information arrived via my internal knowing. For me, this was just another normal day, no different from riding my bike, playing with friends, and eating lunch. I was intuitively aware, which is easy when you are a kid with no opinions, assumptions, or agendas about a person. My observation was completely neutral, and I was seeing his wholeness.

My mother found it comical that I was so candid. After the party, she described his life experiences and that validated my insights. Of course, I wasn't trying to be funny. I was giving him a healing by letting him know that I saw the real him, instead of the intellectual identity he used as a shield to emotionally survive and get the job done. I offered him what I'd received through my near-death experience, the knowledge that we are much more than what shows on the outside. Wasn't that what everyone was seeking?

Turns out, while everyone unconsciously wants to be seen, fear keeps many from consciously experiencing it. People take different roads and run on their own timeframes. Everyone has free will, but, like a closed hand, you can't give someone what they don't want to receive. Since then, I've learned a lot about who is ready for that kind of soul communication.

> ***Knowing where and when to apply your abilities is essential.***

I assumed anyone would be delighted that someone saw them, but he wasn't ready. However, because of that brief exchange, he always appreciated me, even if he didn't fully understand why. All my childhood experiences with intuition were like this. In my mind, those interactions were normal and routine, even my near-death experience. Only later when I received intensive training did I understand the value of what I'd known and experienced as a child.

When my daughter was five, we had our annual costume party and she dressed as a tree goddess. With her wand, she went through the guests cheerfully saying, "I'll turn you back into yourself!" Children know how to be fully themselves without a veneer. Their radiant presence invites others to recollect their sacred origins, feel joy, and just be themselves. This was my daughter's way of saying *Hello* and validating each person's brightest capability. Like a tree effortlessly accessing the mycelia, she connected partygoers from different backgrounds, ages, and cultures.

Remembering who you are is an endless journey of returning to yourself, to be yourself.

Intuitive Tools

Activity 1
Golden Sun: Say Hello to Yourself through Creative Visualization

This creative visualization activity helps you say *Hello* to your inner knowing, set your energy with qualities that support you, and harmonize your soul-body team. Your aim is to recognize and remember those bright, infinite, clear, and capable intuitive qualities that are often overshadowed by your intellectual mind. Creative visualization engages your imagination to have a new experience in any area where you're ready for an upgrade, healing, or emotional reset.

This activity sends a clear signal that you choose to empower your life experiences outside of the intellect. Learning to access and apply visualization is an explorative, experiential work in progress, not something that comes together perfectly in one day. This activity is the foundation of many other activities in this book, so practice saying *Hello* to your body and your infinite light every single day! There are two ways to use Golden Suns as an intuitive tool in your daily life: By visualizing filling yourself with pure golden sun energy (your life force energy) or to set your energy through imagining golden suns full of specific qualities that you love.

Directions

1. Sit comfortably in a chair with both feet on the floor. Give yourself total permission to have fun through experiencing your awareness engaged in creative action in this moment.
2. Start conscious breathing. While breathing, notice if you unconsciously "take" a breath, as if there's not enough, or if you consciously "give" yourself a deep breath. This has a different quality of energy that signals to your body you have all you need. *Give* yourself three conscious breaths.
3. Visualize a bright ball of energy above your head, an enormous divine golden sun filled with light, life force, and healing energy optimized just for you.

4. Put qualities you love into this ball of overflowing life force energy that you'd like to consciously experience or cultivate in greater abundance within your mind. (Examples: receptivity, creativity, curiosity, appreciation, laughter, imagination, self-love, self-trust, space to be yourself.)
5. Allow this life force energy to saturate you from head to toe, and then let it flow outside your body, filling your egg-shaped energy field extending three to four feet around you, including above your head and below your feet, saturating every part of your physical and nonphysical space. Experience your healing life force energy and your creative power.
6. Give yourself total permission to receive this healing energy. Celebrate your choice!
7. Be curious and practice observing your energy field around you filled with golden suns. Stretch your arms out and slowly bring your hands toward your body, noticing any differences in the energy quality, density, or frequency around you. See how this energy is beyond any mental, emotional, or physical restrictions or confinements.
8. Say *Hello* to your physical body.
9. Now say *Hello* to your bright soul presence.
10. Observe if you experience a vibrational frequency difference between saying *Hello* to your physical body and saying *Hello* to your soul presence. There is a difference in the density, frequency, or quality.
11. Once more say *Hello* to your physical body. Tell your body: "I love you. You're safe. We can be a harmonious team." Now say *Hello* to your bright soul presence again.

Activity 2
Your Intuitive Origin Story

Building upon the Golden Sun activity and from this place of *Hello*, apply visualization to remember clues, symbols, and memories from your intuitive origin story. Origin stories, like the story of your birth, contain data and details that can be confirmed and defined. Your intuitive origin story, however, is beyond your intellect. This story can have layers of meaning that are not necessarily definable to anyone but you. Through intuition-based tools, writing, meditation, art, or movement, you will access your earliest experiences of being more than your body or intellect. This sacred origin story is your personal truth, validating what you know when you access your limitless awareness.

Directions

1. Sit comfortably in a chair with both feet on the floor.
2. Give yourself three conscious breaths. Say Hello to your body, and your bright soul presence.
3. Following the Golden Sun activity, visualize a ball of light above your head that is an enormous golden sun, filled with infinite light, and life force healing energy. Put qualities you love into this ball of limitless light like receptivity, creativity, curiosity, appreciation, laughter, self-love, space to be yourself, and self-acceptance. Imagine this light within and surrounding you like a giant egg (see Chapter 1, Activity 1).
4. Invite your awareness to give you any clues, symbols, awareness, or memories about your intuitive origin story. Alternatively, write, meditate, doodle, paint, dance, walk in the woods, compose a song on your guitar, or use any other method to remember clues, symbols, qualities, or memories about your origins.
5. You can visualize your origin story like a movie, as if you're looking at a screen inside your head.
6. Notice if your intellect discounts what arises. This is a clue that you are on the right track. Stay true to your intuitive course.
7. Discern any changes in temperature, brightness, colors, qualities, sounds, and feelings that arise when you experience your

story from this energetic space of limitless imagination. Notice how you feel or what you just "know" when you envision your origin story.
8. After practicing this exercise, write down (or speak into voice notes) your experience and any associative visions, knowing, sounds, images, qualities, or senses.
9. Validate the truth of your own knowledge of yourself.
10. Before bed, ask for messages that, upon waking, will help you remember yourself beyond your physical body.
11. Share your intuitive origin story with a trusted friend or partner, if that feels correct.

Chapter Two
Bookmarked Pictures in Your Mind

Before you say a word, your mind creates an image which then becomes a thought. Like a movie inside your head, your mind constantly projects bookmarked pictures from your past experiences, including your thoughts and feelings associated with them. This is your overthinking mind in action. For example, think of the word *school* and you'll bring up thousands of images associated with that word, some conscious and some unconscious. Your creative power runs the movie projector.

Why does one person stress about something, but another person in the exact same situation does not? Your friend is relaxed about getting dental work, but dentists terrify you, and you don't know exactly why. You're comfortable advocating for your child's needs at school, but your friend gets frazzled about it. You breeze through a work presentation, but your brother gets overwhelmed, even though you grew up in the same family, and your parents are comfortable with public speaking. You feel stressed when you interact with a certain family member or colleague, while others don't seem bothered by them at all, even when the person's behavior stays exactly the same. You like traveling to far-off places, but your friend, for no apparent reason, is afraid to fly. She doesn't even know why she gets nervous.

When I first moved to the United States, my family bought land before we arrived but didn't yet have money to build a house on it.

We moved into tents in the March snow on our property. We built a little lean-to and cooked our meals over an open fire. I had my own tent with all my stuffed animals on one side. I was living an absolutely fantastic adventure. We had no electricity, phone, or shower, but my sister and I had a rope swing to play on and trees to climb.

Years later, I mentioned this to someone, and they immediately reacted by saying, "Oh that must have been so traumatic for you!" I was momentarily stunned. That's when I realized how everyone holds such different pictures about what constitutes suffering or hardship, trauma or fun, or what they believe "not enough" means. That's one way we all live in different realities. We even project pictures onto others that don't resonate for them. Neutrality is far more valuable and creates space for deeper insight.

As a child, I read the energy and pictures of my parents in action as they expressed their enthusiasm, adaptability, courage, intelligence, humor, and creativity. Each step of the way, they envisioned a new life and created it. I naturally matched the energy they were setting and expressing. I watched people who had lived in our rural community for many generations show up to help us new people build a house together.

> ***Bookmarked pictures are completely subjective and often become the window through which you view life.***

Everyone relates to themselves and to each other through these image projections and patterns. I could have experienced living in a tent in the March snow as a negative experience, but to me it was fun. At the same time, at my new elementary school, kids asked, "Why do you have a weird accent?" In my new culture, my social survival goal was to *not* stand out. Yet I kept standing out anyway! Years later, as a teen, someone said to me, "You're weird." Hilariously, that simple comment hit me like a ton of bricks. If I didn't update my unconscious energy in relationship to that word, I would miss valuable opportunities to speak my truth in beneficial ways because I'd be focused on trying not to stand out. Shifting this was more than just thinking about it, it was a matter of deciding to disengage my energy or power I'd invested in that simple, relatively mundane word. Everyone I've encountered as a teacher has plenty of words like this in their mind, often unconscious, that cause an unwanted reaction. Your conscious awareness brings neutrality to these words so that you don't waste time and energy getting stuck on a feeling. *Isn't that an old song?*

Decades later, can't you still feel the emotions from certain movie scenes? Your bookmarked pictures engage your creative power and cause you to react, even when you don't like it, when it causes stress, overwhelm, self-doubt, anger, guilt, avoidance, fear, or other emotions. These unconscious patterns affect the way you relate to yourself and your world. They have an enormous effect on the quality of your daily life and relationships. For example, you might genuinely believe that you are not good at something when you are actually much better than you think and miss an opportunity to use that skill to help others.

Your intuitive awareness can be a powerful ally for dissolving these patterns, especially for dysfunctional images that get in the way of living your best life. When you become aware of intuitive tools and use them, you can free yourself and create space to imagine new experiences. When applied correctly, this juncture of active imagination, intuition, and creativity can calm your overthinking mind and offer you freedom of choice.

Learning the Power of Conscious Choice through Bee Stings

As detailed in chapter one, I nearly died from anaphylactic shock from a bee sting at age four. After that, when a bee buzzed around me, I'd get nervous and run away even when it was only a yellow jacket that I intellectually knew wasn't interested in me. I could tell myself I was safe over and over, but that made no difference. My bookmarked pictures were more powerful than the caption underneath the bee, saying: Don't worry, you're okay.

This is a great example of how influential bookmarked pictures can be. You are often unaware of pictures that fuel your behavior, thoughts, judgments, opinions, or feelings. When you finally realize what's happening, you feel amazed and liberated.

Unlike a bee sting, most bookmarked pictures are more subtle. For example, when you're in first grade, you have a whole bunch of pictures that you don't have in tenth grade, such as what you consider to be interesting or delicious. Yet, just like my "weird" example, some subtle pictures remain just under the surface. They will surprise you when you finally notice them and gratefully release them. Suddenly, you no longer criticize yourself about some aspect of your body, or you no longer get stuck comparing yourself to someone who seems to have a better career or lifestyle.

As an adult, I learned intuitive tools that helped me find these bookmarked pictures, so I can support myself and others in releasing them. When you heal your bookmarked pictures, you update your operating system.

> **Bookmarked pictures, especially fearful ones, keep you invested in the past.**

On the one hand, my bee-sting experience was a pivotal moment for my spiritual growth and conscious awareness. After all, it was the *Hello* that reminded me I was much more than a four-year-old body.

Still, my body said, *Do not let that happen again! Run!* Fear makes you want to flee, whether physically, emotionally, or mentally. This can be very subtle or extremely obvious. Your brain tries to keep you safe by replaying all the scary times of your life, so you do not repeat dangerous experiences. Bookmarked pictures cause knee-jerk reactions, procrastination, or avoidance instead of discerning responses. These misplaced reactions take away your creative freedom of choice. Fear aims you toward resistance or judgment of your aversions which stops or slows your healing. Love is pure energy and doesn't resist anything. Moving out of fear energy gives you space to heal. A golden sun full of self-love can be an effortless antidote for fear energy.

> **When you are in fear, you might have what you think is an intuitive feeling about something or someone when you are actually on a nervous-system feedback loop.**

Later in life, I realized that at the time of the bee-sting event, I unconsciously internalized others' fear pictures and felt their fear as if it were actually mine, which made the trauma worse.

As an aware, sensitive child, I could not always discern which feelings, opinions, or thoughts were mine. I was like a ham radio, tuned into many frequencies. I couldn't always understand all the information input and effectively manage the energy of it by consciously releasing it. I wanted to improve conditions around me and help everyone to heal, so I unconsciously collected extra input and carried it with me. This is what happens when you're not fully aware of being intuitive, and you care deeply about the well-being of others. We don't always know what is really us because we mix our genuine feelings with absorbed emotions, and we use those mixed feelings to make things real for us. Our pure and simple awareness guides us to see through, sort through, and recognize what is true and aligned for us. Through our awareness we can also tap into feelings that nourish us, or that we didn't know we had, or that inspire creative expression.

Over time I observed that many people had lost sight of an incredibly healing and powerful relationship within themselves, their intuitive awareness. Restoring this relationship begins with observing it and saying *Hello*.

As a child I spent a lot of time exploring with my sister and on my own in the natural world on our farm, which gave me freedom to imagine and space to observe. I observed that just as everything in the natural world is intricately interrelated (plants, soil, water, air, animals), we are also living in relationship with our intuitive awareness, consciously or unconsciously. When I was fearful or worried, I envisioned putting my fear into a bubble and making the bubble evaporate. No one taught me to do that. My imagination engaged my creative power to manage my fears through visualization. As an adult, I learned this as an intuitive tool, visualizing a rose or bubble. (I never had a name for it before.)

> **Because intuition is innate, it made sense to me that intuitive tools are also innate. They help us become more consciously aware, which is experiential rather than intellectual.**

My childhood visualization helped me to recognize that fear might "sit on you," but that's a different experience than when you "become it." You can have space from your fear. Maybe that is why long ago we used to say, "Anger is upon you," or "Fear is upon me." It's passing, not an identity. In modern English we say, *I am* fearful. *You are* scared, a subtle difference but so important.

My bookmarked picture of a bee equaled possible death, so it was a hardwired reaction pattern. That event held so much energy, its effects took longer to release. By the time I was sixteen, I'd been stung many times without any anaphylactic reaction and finally released my bookmarked pictures of bees. From this neutral place, I could respond rather than react from survival. Releasing that picture rewired my nervous system. When that fear cleared out of my space, a whole bunch of other seemingly unrelated fears also departed, permanently. This is because as unconscious energy, one fear easily attracts or connects to another fear. My hardwired pattern was actually changeable. By applying my creative power to heal myself, I updated my relationship to that fear. At that time, I had few intuitive tools for this process, so it took twelve years. With practiced awareness, you won't have to wait that long.

Shedding Fear as a Route to Healing

Bookmarked pictures related to fear are a big force in your life. Just watch the news or social media and you'll get a giant dose of fear energy. We often push down fear so it doesn't overwhelm us. Even so, if you match or resist fear energy, you're likely to absorb some of it and perceive its effects as your own. Your nervous system signals anxiety or stress to your body, which confirms the fear as real, even when it came from the news or from a family member or friend.

That's why you could suddenly become scared of flying, or phobic of nonpoisonous snakes or swimming, without a bad experience. Because of absorbing outside generalized fear energy, you might start worrying about something out of the blue without an intuitive message. When you heal yourself, you release nonspecific fear energy that came from your environment.

Imagine a core fear (metaphorically) like a "fear corporation" with the CEO at the center, surrounded by hundreds of smaller fears all serving the CEO. Shine your bright light on the CEO, say *Hello*, and recognize, "Oh that's just an old picture," and the whole construct crumbles, simultaneously dissolving many random smaller fears that worked for the CEO.

If you are safe, but you still have fear bombarding you, eventually you may stop trusting your intuitive knowing. I tried to tell my reasoning self to stand calmly next to a bee at a picnic, but my feeling self wouldn't listen until I released the bookmarked picture holding the fear energy and updated my nervous system. Each time an update happens, you free yourself from the limitations in those pictures. Your creative power, your light, is no longer empowering those pictures, and you can welcome more of your creative energy back to you in the present. You will remember your old fear stories, but they no longer control you. You can be neutral in that area.

By steadily and gently releasing fear energy, you can follow a compassionate route to healing. This isn't a quick fix that happens in one day. It's like clearing a toxin out of your system or taking a new step to improve your daily fitness. If you try to do it all in one week or month, you may end up walking away before you feel the joy of success. It's worth reminding yourself that although we are all trained to compete in many areas of life, healing isn't a competition and less is more. The old pictures rise to the surface and are on their way out, but they need to be given space to release, and the effort of competition (force) makes them stick. The intellect can easily confuse healing that happens within your mind as a problem that needs to be solved or controlled. Healing is really a cause for celebration because you have more space and freedom now. Your loving and compassionate inner permission will gracefully allow this celebration to happen with spacious orchestration.

Set aside your assumptions and give yourself permission to observe what pops up in your mind. Say *Hello* to the bright, free, spacious power of your inner knowing, innovativeness, and imagination. Each time you become aware of pictures associated with your emotions, reactions, and thoughts, your awareness alone can free you from a disempowering pattern. This is why exploring your intuitive awareness is so much fun! When you feel confined by the quiet, in-the-background concerns of worry, stress, guilt, procrastination, or self-judgment, turn to your bright awareness.

Energy as a Vibrational Frequency

When you become aware of your relationship to the images swirling in your overthinking mind, you open a doorway to transform your daily experience of life. The key to the door is learning to consciously relate to energy as a vibrational frequency.

What is energy? Well, everything! We all have an energetic blueprint or signature. Everything, everyone, and every experience vibrates at a certain speed, known as its frequency. The only difference between one thing and another is its vibrational frequency.

> ***Energy isn't bad or good. It's simply a vibrational frequency to be observed.***

You may notice that happy, loving, or enthusiastic experiences make you feel empowered. This is high-vibration energy. At this frequency, you might sing, laugh, or try something new. You could experience this frequency as brightness, space, and freedom. Whether you did it consciously or unconsciously, you engaged with this frequency.

On the other hand, when you engage with resentment, fear, guilt, worry, self-judgment, or control, you are at a different frequency. You may feel closed down and tight with limited choices. Perhaps you temporarily withdraw from others by either shutting down or going on a random tangent. Maybe you dig into your bookmarked pictures as a reaction to these vibrational frequencies and think repetitive negative thoughts. This is low-frequency energy.

Reading Energy

Once, I was at a party chatting with an acquaintance I'd seen infrequently over the years. I would normally describe him as content or jolly, but on this day his energy had changed dramatically. I couldn't help but "see" that he was sitting under a lot of grief and loss. What happened to cause this change in his energy? Had he lost a parent?

We were not close friends, so I wasn't about to ask, yet I cared about this person's well-being. I turned my intuitive awareness toward my question and read his energy. I saw that he was going through a difficult breakup from a long-term relationship. I couldn't directly offer him help, since he wasn't open to working with me. Instead, I imagined this person in a bright golden bubble, full of his own life force energy, feeling lighthearted and creative.

I didn't match his suffering and add my own bookmarked pictures of yet more suffering. Anytime you imagine the suffering of another, you can't fully know their unique experience. All you can do is create your own version of it and build on it in your mind in a way that can be inaccurate. Instead, I felt compassion and visualized his innate power to heal. Compassion is being present and aware that someone suffers without matching or becoming the suffering.

I imagined a favorable outcome for him. He would choose to go there in his own time, in his own way, in alignment with his own truth.

Perhaps he would unconsciously match my joyful energy and take a step upward in his vibrational frequency. I had certainly experienced that when I was feeling down and a friend showed up from a different frequency to make me laugh: This was an invitation for me to change my energy.

A year later, we happened to be at another party, chatting about rising house prices. He was clearly doing well then. His energy had changed immensely. He briefly mentioned how he had to sell his house due to a relationship breakup. He got a great price for it and eventually found an even better house with a barn for an art studio. Finally, he had manifested a place for his long-held creative hobby.

Places affect you energetically, too. When you walk into a building, what you like or dislike can be more about the energy of the space than the furnishings.

Imagine the vibrational frequencies of an ordinary situation such as going to the dentist. You might like the energy at the dentist's office because you experience an invisible quality of safety. If the office is physically unappealing, you might become aware that your sense of it is clearly not about the waiting room couch or the decor. Oh wait, is it the energy of the cheerful receptionist? Or maybe it's the dentist, because she has a lovely sense of humor. She's compassionate and hears you.

Imagine this dentist's waiting room is a beautiful space, but you do not like the vibe. You experience the space as tired, tense, or chaotic. Maybe the hygienist tells you all his woes while cleaning your teeth. That frequency makes you feel awkward or uncomfortable because you already feel tense with your teeth being scraped. Maybe his woes match your own, and your mind travels into your file of bookmarked pictures. Disturbing *what-ifs* come over you. Suddenly, you are worrying about your child at school, for no specific reason.

If the dentist barely seems to notice you have a body outside of your teeth, your bookmarked pictures might highlight how your basketball coach made you feel unseen in sixth grade. But this time, you suddenly become aware of it and say to yourself, *What? I'm still holding on to that old invalidating energy?* You start to laugh within and, *Boom!* that picture no longer directs your feelings. That's how to break the pattern. Fear keeps you resistant. Love, laughter, appreciation, willingness, and even curiosity change your energy frequency.

Energy can make you feel jazzed up and mentally sharp, or it can make you spacey, irritated, overwhelmed, and a thousand other possibilities. You respond to energy in your own unique ways. Whether conscious or unconscious, everything is a relationship and offers an opportunity for you to become aware of the vibrational frequencies in your world. This can happen without doing anything more than observing like when you are taking a walk, and you decide to become aware of something you never noticed before. It's quite fun, once you make it so!

Energy Reactions, Images, and Your Nervous System

Your nervous system is always matching your experiences with bookmarked pictures to protect you and ensure your survival. Most of the time, this occurs on a microlevel, so it's not as obvious as a trauma event. For example, a person who wants to socialize more but finds themselves avoiding fun events because they can't get into the mindset to enjoy it. Or someone who would like to grow their business but ends up scrolling on social media instead, falling into procrastination caused by hidden fear pictures that say, "Don't bother, it's not worth it."

You might misinterpret information that doesn't fit with what's established in your nervous system. As you develop more intuitive awareness, you rewire yourself and harness the power of your creativity in updated ways. You start to see what you were unaware of, both on a physical and nonphysical level. When this happens, you become empowered for your evolution, well-being, and happiness.

You can choose to create from the vibrational frequency of fear, doubt, and worry, or you can create from the energy of compassion, joy, and generosity. In one day, you may move from one frequency to another. Everyone has low-frequency days. After all, we do live in a world of duality! You can gain strength by realizing you have more creative power than you think, literally. You can transform your inner landscape in an instant.

Misdirected Creative Energy

You express your creative power through your physical body—verbally and nonverbally—whether you are expressing or receiving information. Your awareness helps you discern if you love a specific energy or not. If not, you can unsubscribe.

If you hang out with people who express negative or perfectionistic attitudes, you might naturally start acting or feeling like them in subtle ways, or you might resist them. You unconsciously absorb feelings that you don't like when you resist them. Then, you unintentionally express those feelings toward another person. The other person picks up on that energy because they're intuitive and sensitive, too.

Have you ever noticed how enthusiastic you feel after listening to an inspiring podcast or having a delightful conversation with a friend? Based on your bookmarked pictures, you unconsciously match with high- or low-frequency energy around you—whether you like the energy or not. The way you empower these high and low vibrational frequencies creates any number of possible outcomes.

When you create something in resistance to low vibrational energies, you might wonder why the result is out of line with your true voice, personality, or path in life. It's easy for vibrational frequency chain reactions to bounce back and forth between people.

You can find a thousand examples of what happens when humans interact in spaces with lots of other people (i.e., workplaces, institutions, or organizations). You can intentionally apply your energy toward incredible team building and collaboration that brings everyone together, or you can focus your energy on gossip or trying to control something you don't like. Energy gets collected and shared. Since energy is nonverbal and unseen, this usually happens unconsciously.

Own Your Creative Power

Remember that you are a powerful, expressive being. Redirect your attention from overthinking reactions to aware responses.

> *You are always creating, so become aware of what you would like to consciously create.*

Walk into any meeting, classroom, hospital, office building, landscape, park, or house and notice how the energy is different from place to place. Do you like some of those places better than others? You might find it easy to name the quality of the energy. Other times, you don't have a name for it. Can you be neutral to it, or does it throw you off? As a conscious director, you can become more neutral with practice.

If you're not neutral in a space, observe what your reaction is in different spaces. One person might try to control the space to feel safe, which isn't ideal for other people sharing the space. Another person might avoid it altogether missing out on valuable opportunities like the dinner party they wanted to attend. Another person might resist the space, becoming temporarily difficult to be around. That's why neutrality is a tool of consciousness with unlimited benefits and applications. It gives you and others space to be, simultaneously.

You can relate to energy in dozens of ways. You can react to it from bodily instinct or respond gently to it after an observational pause. You might also *become* the energy and lose track of where or who you are. You could laugh it off or override it and compartmentalize it. Other times, you might try to overpower it. However, when you resist, you are adding your energy to it, and it will grow. What you resist persists.

Have a conversation with a stranger and notice if you enjoy it or not. That's all energy. You experience that person's frequency in relation to your own. Every time you feel irritated or enthralled with someone or something, you are experiencing a matching of their energy with yours. Sometimes you have a good match, and sometimes you don't.

You affect others with your creative power. Even without speaking, a conversation between you and somebody else can go on in your mind in pictures or internal words. This relationship affects your vibrational frequency.

> *Nonverbal communication still consists of your creative power because it contains your bookmarked pictures and emotions.*

When you try to avoid discomfort, you often do not speak your mind, right? Yet this avoidance usually takes far more energy from you than if you actually communicated. Whenever you communicate your creative power in a beneficial way, you make an enormous positive impact in the world, beyond what you might realize. As you bring consciousness to your bookmarked pictures, this new awareness positively affects the vibrational frequency of those around you. The correct application of your powerful energy can change everything, but only you can know when this application should take place.

Changing Your Bookmarked Patterns

Once you become more aware of your interactions with energies in your everyday life, you can apply the power of your creative energy and flip the switch from low to high frequency. Step out of the old patterns and bookmarked pictures, and you'll support your life in new ways.

While you can't always immediately switch out unpleasant circumstances and make them positive, with your practiced awareness you can transform and empower yourself from within. Once you acknowledge that, you won't need to run from your outer circumstances as often. Going back to the dentist example, you can transform your inner experience of the dentist appointment, even though the energy is not exactly what you like. You can become more neutral. Of course, you can always change dentists!

As an example of dropping bookmarked pictures that no longer serve you, you might want to change jobs because of a negative workplace vibe. After thinking it over, you realize that you actually like most people in your workplace. The one exception is your boss. Although you don't recognize this at first, he brings up a bookmarked picture of your father when you were school aged.

Your dad wanted you to get more exercise, so he tried to force you to participate in sports when you were interested in art. This invalidated your creativity, so whenever this boss comes around, your bookmarked picture immediately drops your energy. Your creative power lights up the old images of that past experience. This causes you to feel like you can't express yourself. The outcome of this low-frequency vibration is that you hold back your most helpful creative ideas because you fear judgment.

One day while on a lunch break, you walk in the park and from your intuitive knowing you finally understand what's happening within. You release the old pictures and become neutral. You make a new choice. At the next work meeting, you voice your creative ideas. Your boss listens and gives it an enthusiastic thumbs-up! *Bingo*, your relationship with this person gets brighter and more open. You see each other more clearly.

> **Communication conflicts often happen when two people have the same bookmarked pictures, although they appear different at first.**

In this work example, when you updated your past energy, your self-image changed and so did your image of your boss. His pictures of you likely changed as well when he saw you express more of the real you. Feeling seen increases your confidence to communicate more in the future as your inner trust grows. This combination starts an upward spiral of positive energy and opens space for ever-greater creative collaboration. Both of you released old pictures and experienced more space and fresh energy to create a higher vibration experience. Healing happens!

This inner transformation goes beyond your relationship with your boss. It also changes the way you relate with others, including your dad. You realize he wasn't trying to invalidate your creativity. He wanted to make you physically fit because he felt that was his responsibility. He didn't understand the type of creative validation you needed because he too had not received that type of *Hello* as a child.

Although you may not know what your boss's deeper matching pictures are with you, most people have matching pictures about not being fully seen for who they are. People also commonly share matching pictures about invalidation, sometimes in unexpected or subtle ways. It is no surprise that many people from all walks of life feel unseen and invalidated in a culture where we are not taught to say *Hello* to what is infinite and bright within one another. We're taught to look at only the cover.

When you match energy with others, you can have either a response (conscious) or a reaction (unconscious), both of which can either repel or attract the people around you. By noticing what happens, you can choose how you'd like to interact with them. That's a game changer—an instant healing!

> **Only one person needs to be aware in order to transform the entire relationship. This is even more powerful when both people are aware.**

Through your conscious awareness, you saw how a bookmarked picture created an obstacle at your job. Then, you stepped outside the data template for a moment and saw beyond your limitations. In a thinking-dominant culture, you were not taught to do this. Yet this ability is innate to you. As a creative being, you can choose to live in the present instead of the past. Releasing pictures lets this happen more often.

If you're reading this book, you are intuitive and you are a healer yet the two are not separate. As a child your first healing project was your family. This is why I have always told my daughter, "If you see something that you dislike about the way that we as your parents are creating, relating, or navigating then you'd be wise to just unmatch from it rather than become or resist it. If you see something that you love about the way we are creating, relating, or navigating, now that's worth matching and learning from!" This gives her conscious permission to have more space to be herself and distinguish her energy from our energy. In her relationships with others this awareness gives her clarity that allows her to make choices from her own authentic energy. For example, she chooses not to get distracted trying to fix unsolvable problems which can show up in a thousand subtle forms like people pleasing or getting entangled in drama. Differentiating our energy from that of our parents is both a game changer and also a subtle work in progress for everyone. There will always be times when we accidentally match energy that we dislike, or get sidelined by drama or unsolvable problems, but with practiced, conscious awareness we can vastly shift our daily ratio!

Creating from the Present

Although you can access all your wisdom gained from the past, you actually create in the present. You might know this intellectually but have limiting patterns from prior experiences that pop up in specific areas where you have set your sights. When you live in the past or in the future, you can feel like you're spinning your wheels, waiting for something better to happen to you. You can get stuck in pictures and energy that cause you to doubt your ability to create a better life.

By bringing conscious awareness to your bookmarked pictures and the reactions that go with them, you will start to recognize them and say *Hello*. This can happen while you're having conversations with family and friends, exercising, grocery shopping, or working with colleagues. Your intuitive self steps outside of your intellectual framework to distinguish between what's present and what's no longer present.

Every time you heal an old pattern by bringing awareness to it, more of your creativity becomes available in that area. This can positively impact your relationships as well. Intuitive awareness is an unlimited space of discovery. It opens doors for you to consciously express what is true to you and create a far different quality, result, or expression than you'll have from energy absorbed from the outside world. The more awareness you have, the more you can focus your energy on things that bring you joy and inspire solutions.

One of my students, a healthcare professional and writer, recently emailed me to share her appreciation for the creative inner growth she has been having. She said, "Each day has offered new opportunities to release pictures around all the areas of my life where creativity has been blocked. In addition, it's shifted my perceptual awareness; things look a little different, like I have a big scope on things. The creative problem-solving comes from everywhere instead of a narrow perspective. It's super cool. Thanks! Really enjoying 'seeing' this one play out!"

Visualize and Self-Heal

Bookmarked pictures with their unconscious patterns are there for you to heal and release. This can happen naturally as you observe the pictures enough to know that they may not actually be you. When you realize that, perhaps, not all your feelings and thoughts are yours, you can begin to ask, *Is this my energy?*

As a human, you have a habit of thinking you are every emotion and thought that dances around you. In a thinking-dominant culture, you were taught to possess your feelings, rather than witness them without jumping into them. Give yourself space to become aware of where to invest your personal power and energy.

The first step to welcoming your intuitive awareness is opening your curiosity and enthusiasm for observing bookmarked pictures because they show you what you'd like to heal or transform. If you approach this like a serious self-improvement project, your effort will close down your energy for exploration, imagination, and inspiring discovery.

Allow your inner knowing to access the bookmarked pictures associated with a situation. You might have a visual image, or you might not. It doesn't matter either way. Give yourself space to just know. Be the natural curious observer you are! Make new choices and update your life. Stay away from assumptions and trust yourself to know without going into effort (forcing it) to change anything.

Once you let go of a set of interconnected, bookmarked pictures, you can more easily heal whatever pattern resulted from it. This gives you calm, creativity, and control in that specific area of your life. You'll soon feel happier, safe, free, balanced, and clear seeing. You rewired yourself. This increases your intuitive discernment in that area, so you can distinguish between what truly matters and what doesn't matter.

This release is like stepping out of a movie into the sunshine: You'll have more freedom to choose what's most aligned for you. You'll be able to identify strengths that may have been overshadowed before. You may even notice that some aspect of your identity can now be updated, so you're no longer living through that set of reactions.

Then, when you recognize bookmarked pictures, you'll have freedom to respond rather than react. I call this positive growth. This is always a work in progress and never about seeking perfection or completion. That's why life is called a journey. We are all spiritual explorers having a human experience, and there is always a learning curve.

Intuitive Tools

Activity 1
Popping Bubbles: Visualizing Positive Outcomes

This creative visualization activity guides you to release bookmarked pictures that may surface as you imagine new experiences. It will help reset your feelings and overall approach, or it can support you to express yourself in a fresh, updated way. This will give you practice in recognizing that you can release pictures (emotions, opinions, directives, thoughts, etc.) while you are producing something new, healing yourself, or during your busy day. You'll be able to intuitively know, "It's just a picture. It's just energy," so you can unsubscribe from it whenever you like. Releasing bookmarked pictures is deeply healing and allows you to manifest in areas where you are ready for growth or change. You will use this tool throughout the book, and I will refer to it as Popping Bubbles. If you prefer, you can visualize a rose in any color instead of a bubble, each time I refer to Popping Bubbles.

Directions

1. Sit comfortably in a chair with both feet on the floor.
2. Give yourself three conscious breaths.
3. Think of a word. Observe what images pop up in your mind when you think of that word. Validate that you are observing pictures in your mind.
4. Now imagine an upcoming event or situation that causes worry, self-doubt, or stress. For example, you might focus on an important work presentation or a tough conversation with a loved one.
5. Give yourself permission to say *Hello* to your bright soul presence, your body, and your creative power, in order to experience this event in a new light, literally!
6. In your mind's eye, or while imagining it on a movie screen, visualize the entire experience as if it's happening in the present, one moment at a time. Distinguish how you navigate the potential rough patches, as well as the easy interactions.
7. Give yourself 100 percent inner permission to visualize a beneficial outcome. This may be something you haven't consciously imagined yet. Be open to this possibility.
8. Observe what pops up for you during this visualization. Do any pictures or energies show up as self-doubt, worries, fear, annoyance, or resistance? Is your overthinking mind throwing repetitive chatter, old memories or images from the past, self-judgments, uninvited opinions, or invalidations of your creativity and power? Has your energy dropped, and you don't have enough enthusiasm to continue creating your visualization?
9. If this happens, envision an enormous bubble (or rose) that's outside of your personal space.

10. Let the unwanted images, emotions, opinions, or thoughts jump into the bubble (or rose). Watch the images in that bubble (or rose), as if you are sitting in a theater watching a movie.
11. Validate your awareness and your creative power to transform.
12. Pop the bubble (or rose) and watch it totally evaporate, along with all the unwanted images, thoughts, opinions, etc.
13. Visualize a ball of light above your head that is an enormous golden sun, filled with life force healing energy to replenish you. (See Chapter 1, Activity 1 for more details.) Each time you release energy that's not yours, you have created more space for you, so filling it with golden sun replenishes you with your own energy.
14. Choose three qualities or more of energy that you'd like to give yourself, to update your new relationship with yourself in this situation *now*. (Peace, laughter, clarity, etc.)
15. Put these qualities into your golden sun and saturate your entire body and energy field around you with these qualities. Enjoy refreshing yourself from head to toe (and around you) with your own healing energy.
16. Once again, in your mind's eye, visualize the entire upcoming event as if it's happening in present time, one moment at a time. Discern if you feel more spacious, free, enthusiastic, humorous, or empowered in your creative visualization of the upcoming event and consciously cultivate positive feelings about it. If more pictures rise to the surface, repeat steps 8 through 11.
17. Continue to practice your visualization until you fully envision a beneficial outcome that enhances the quality of your life.

Activity 2
Your Inner Self-Permission Meter

Have you ever made a vow to change a pattern that limits you and no longer serves you, only to have it return again and again like a giant pinball machine? With empowered self-permission, you can change your mind when a pattern derails your peace and your goals in life.

If the baseline of your inner self-permission meter is unconsciously low, you can try to make all the changes you like, and yet never seem to reach your goals. In this activity, give yourself 100 percent full permission to change the channel to something you're inspired to create, be, or do. Over time, you can become more aware and increase the levels of your permission meter in areas such as self-care, healing, setting healthy boundaries, happier relationships, personal-professional life balance, creativity, speaking your truth, or areas where you seek greater abundance. Say *Hello* to your inner self-permission, and own your ability to imagine, create, and intuit your optimal life as a bright soul presence!

Directions

1. Sit comfortably in a chair with both feet on the floor.
2. Give yourself three conscious breaths.
3. Give yourself permission to say *Hello* to your bright soul presence, your body, and your creative, intuitive power.
4. Visualize a permission meter that is either digital or a classic gauge. This represents your inner level of self-permission. Imagine this gauge ranges from 0-100 percent with 100 percent signifying the highest level.
5. Envision yourself as the creative director of your life, inner growth, choices, power, and creativity. As director, imagine that you have decided to improve all the conditions of your well-being by increasing your inner permission to receive, imagine, and be intuitive in an unlimited way. Intend that this is your foundation to begin updating all the other areas where you are ready for an upgrade.
6. Begin with your permission to receive. What does your gauge say?
7. Decide that your permission to receive can bump up to 100 percent and intuitively see or know how high it goes. If it's not at 100 percent, no problem, this is just your starting point. You can check on this again anytime and repeat the activity.

Become aware of pictures that surface and pop some bubbles (or roses).

8. Now look at your permission to imagine. What does your gauge tell you?
9. Increase this permission level as well. If you become aware of roadblocks to increasing your permission, pop bubbles (or roses.)
10. Last, notice your gauge for allowing your intuitive knowing.
11. Bump up this permission level, and pop bubbles (or roses) for anything that is divisive to this upgrade.
12. You can repeat this activity to increase your permission baseline in these and any areas you would like to upgrade and bring into present time. Popping bubbles or roses (containing pictures as thoughts, opinions, past experiences, invalidations, etc.) increases your permission levels and heals you.
13. Saturate your whole physical and energy space with golden suns full of life force energy, validating your new levels of permission.

Chapter Three
Manage Your Intellect and Overthinking Mind to Have More Fun and Get More Done

You Are Not Your Intellect

The intellect absorbs and retains a lot of necessary information. Giving us essential skills to help us function in the world, it structures our ideas and communication. However, it's not capable of providing higher levels of inner clarity and discernment all by itself. If we just live solely in our intellect or emotions, we have a different experience than if we combine intuitive knowledge with intellect which gives it more range or dynamic awareness, i.e., 360-degree viewing power. Your intuitive knowledge is beyond your age, education, or intellect. In a way, you know more than your intellect. Since we're always thinking, we might as well give our thinking 360-degree viewing power.

Analyze This

You also have an amazing ability to analyze all kinds of information. This analytical processing skill is part of your intellect and can help with decision-making. Not everyone is good at analyzing the same things. Some people are skilled with analyzing mathematics, geology, music, flight patterns, the plot of a novel or movie, bird migration, comedy, human behavioral patterns, energy patterns, or spiritual growth patterns.

Your analyzer works brilliantly, until it doesn't. For example, let's say you're at the start of a twenty-hour road trip, and you need to analyze the best route to go from where you are to where you need to be. It's winter and you'd like to avoid mountain passes, but you'd also like to bypass big cities, because you enjoy quieter roads. This could be a fun job for your analyzer. You start out fresh and clear with a good plan. Then your friend calls to helpfully remind you about a snowstorm that's coming, even though it won't be anywhere near your planned route. Suddenly you hit a bookmarked picture in your mind, a road bump. You start to worry about the trip. On the news, you heard about a family that got stuck in a huge snowstorm in their car, but luckily survived. You have now brought two other ingredients into your recipe: your friend's interest in keeping you safe and fear-focused news. Suddenly you begin analyzing fear, instead of your trip. Fear is such an intense energy; you could analyze it all day!

Bookmarked pictures from the news about other storms are now popping up, left and right. You feel much less enthusiastic, and your energy drops. You stop feeling clear and creative. Worry overload is upon you causing overthinking or overanalyzing. You start to feel doubtful about your route, and it's hard to think straight. It all started the moment you unconsciously matched your friend's fear energy. Then everywhere you looked, there was more fear to match!

Your analyzer is a tremendously useful tool. Yet if you're unaware of the way you relate with it, it will try to analyze both useful and not useful stuff, depending on what scroll you feed it or what emotions you have absorbed from many other sources. Scroll on guilt or resentment, and it will analyze that. Feed it a brilliant idea from your intuitive knowing that improves the conditions of the world, and it will focus on that!

When the analyzer gets jammed up (like a paper printer), then it cannot work as effectively, clearly, or cleanly in concert with you. Instead of functioning like an ideal collaborative partner, the analyzer instead gets bogged down, diverted, or overwhelmed when it is overloaded with pictures from overthinking. Brain fog can result from a clogged analyzer! When you normally have a decent memory, but suddenly can't remember your phone number, social security number, or other easily remembered things, know that overthinking has jammed up your analyzer.

Once you become aware of the thought debris derailment that happens from overanalyzing, you can have more control over how well your analyzer performs. Your practiced intuitive awareness is the best remedy. Other remedies include tools like bubble popping, or changing gears (like playing with your dog), or exercising to reboot and clear out. You might need a good night's sleep. When you learn to associate the overthinking mind with a cue to manage your intellect and analyzer team, you can rebound much more quickly, and then return to your task.

> **When the intellect and analyzer include intuition, things go even better for you!**

Imagine that you have cleared out your analyzer from the fear pictures collected on the news and finished analyzing your driving route. But there is one section where you can't resolve which way to go, because both ways have pros and cons. You are looking for a fun place to spend the night, but you don't know the area. That's when you can ask your inner guidance which way you'll most enjoy, or which way is safer. Your intuitive awareness is the key to optimizing your thinking, energy, and, ultimately, your choices.

Proving Value through Intellect Starts in School

Our standardized educational system trains you to *become* your intellect, so it is easy to forget that there is enough space for all of you, as the creative and powerful being that you are. Living solely in your intellect equals trading off other valuable aspects of yourself, even sometimes your true feelings, as if they are not comparatively acceptable.

An identity formed by a trade-off causes a funny imbalance in your personal biome. Like a pendulum, your identity swings to either seek or resist approval. Or it just swings back and forth depending on the situation but never finds that balanced sweet spot. Our standardized educational system is set up around competition, based on comparison. You develop coping reactions to protect yourself from feeling not quite enough as you are, like shutting off feelings. Those emotions may not even be yours. If you look intuitively, you can discern.

A type of survival thinking gets established by years of comparing yourself with others. Even when someone says you are intelligent, bright, capable, valuable, and worthy, if you receive this message solely through the filter of your intellect, it will be deflected. This beautiful knowledge will not fully settle within you so you can experience it. The moment you have a little space from that rigid energy, change happens.

> *Your inner knowing gives you a simple, validating message in the space of a moment.*

This message can show up in a hundred different ways, for a million different reasons, but it will never invalidate you or another person. Intuition will never urge you to compete, compare, control, or prove you are worthy or valuable. Intuition is a bridge to greater unity that's always open.

I'm not suggesting that schools shouldn't exist because they focus more on intellect than intuition. Schools provide many valuable intellectual skills and social navigational growth. I just wish the school system validated inner knowing and inner value. So often, children who navigate some academic or emotional challenges are highly intuitive, their creativity is off the charts, and they are picking up on everyone else's energy. Without validation of their brightest capability, children can get stuck on negative self-worth pictures, self-doubt pictures, or other struggles. The fastest way out of that conundrum is saying *Hello* to your bright presence, which is truly incomparable because it is a direct experience of your innate and infinite value!

Trading inner knowing for intellect as a child becomes a pattern that can leave many adults with the subtle but familiar feeling of inferiority or "not enoughness." If you make paella but don't add the saffron, something is missing. You only need a little saffron to make all the rest of the ingredients pop and harmonize. Every ingredient is needed for a recipe to be fully expressed. Likewise, you will want to balance your intellect with your intuition.

The Intellect Off Course: Heavy-Duty Overthinkers

Without clear direction, the intellect can veer off into tangents of overthinking or intellectualizing. This is not the same quality of energy as the useful and productive analysis of your driving route.

When unwanted thoughts or emotions show up in the form of bookmarked pictures, as an unconscious survival strategy you may switch to tune-out mode, distraction mode, keep-busy mode, or compartmentalization mode. Being with thoughts you don't want to think about anymore can be a challenge. Inside your head, it can feel like the United Nations trying to negotiate with the ego in favor of human rights and world peace! The battle for world peace is playing out in our minds every day because we are not given tools to find neutrality within ourselves.

> ***Much of what exhausts, overwhelms, stresses, and burns you out is intellectualizing or overthinking what you can't solve, what you feel responsible for, what hurts you, and what you fear.***

Our minds can be on hyperdrive, even while we might appear quiet or calm on the outside. The overthinking mind can sometimes make people feel locked inside their thoughts, unable to express themselves. Others might talk nonstop as a result of their overthinking mind. One of the reasons people like to go on vacation is to get a break from overthinking. Conversely, some people can't take a vacation, because they don't know what to do with their mind if they stop working or overthinking. You can never judge a person by their cover!

It's easiest to judge your own cover, confusing self-critical thinking with critical thinking. You jump onto the hamster wheel of low-frequency, bookmarked patterns, believing you are critically thinking of a solution. In actuality, you are heavy-duty overthinking. Don't add to your self-critical thinking by feeling bad about your overthinking!

Heavy-duty overthinkers can sometimes end up sad, angry, worried, and overwhelmed. They can find themselves in resistance to receiving help, or sitting under the weight of the world that they yearn to fix. It's hard to fix stuff when you're stuck in the middle of patterns that feel unresolvable! The overthinking mind can cause people to overdrink, smoke, take drugs, or drive themselves to keep constantly busy or strive for perfection.

Whenever you notice yourself overthinking, decide to become aware of the energy patterns running your attention, and bring some inner laughter into your mind as an antidote. Use these moments as wonderful opportunities to say *Hello* to your bright awareness and self-love.

> *Add intuitive awareness to your analytical and intellectual thinking and your creativity will come online with transformational solutions.*

Give the Intellect and Analyzer a Direction

Knowing that your intellect likes to have a clear purpose will help create a new experience for you. Compare your intellect with a border collie. I grew up with half a dozen delightful border collies. They are 100 percent working dogs with a herding instinct and a singular goal. If that dog doesn't have the opportunity to fulfill its primary mission of running across a wide-open field joyfully guiding sheep while obeying commands, a border collie will go off on wild tangents. This is not the collie's fault. One of our border collies would chase shadows on the lawn when she wasn't engaged with herding our sheep. That's a great literal and metaphorical image for us humans, wouldn't you agree?

Similarly, you need to give your intellect a clear direction to guide it along its mission. When you recognize your most purposeful creative endeavors from your inner knowing, you can enlist your intellect to help you carry out those tasks to share with the world! If your ideas are delightful, woolly sheep, then with your directives, your intellect can round them up! At every chance, your intellect tries to outthink, out race, and especially, fix. If you do not offer the intellect a way to run across the field of your mind, with succinct guidance, it will randomize. If you doubt this, consider how many mundane tangents you get distracted by in the course of one day.

Undirected by you, the analytical mind can be on overdrive when your intellect has full control. Border collies have the skills to divide up a flock into separate pastures to graze or keep the flock together and herd them into one pasture. Lacking clear direction, they might unnecessarily divide the sheep flock in two halves, going in opposite directions, when they were intended to stay as a united flock. Using an analyzer mind, you command the priority list so that your flock of ideas or collaborative projects doesn't become scattered.

Without your wise inner awareness to collaborate, mediate, moderate, and bring balance, the intellect and analyzer team is compelled to fix or separate everything. Often this involves being *right* about how it *must* be solved. How much of what your intellect wants to resolve is actually yours to even remedy? All of this overthinking costs you extra time, energy, and effort. When you feel compelled to figure out everything or fix everyone, eventually you feel worn out or disillusioned.

> ***Healers, teachers, coaches, change makers, thought leaders, health practitioners, and volunteers, all aiming their sights on giving in a million great ways, are most susceptible to getting stuck into fixing overdrive, which leads to burnout or health issues.***

Are you using your intellect, or is it using you?

The Answers Lie in the Space Between

What's a secret to accessing your intuitive awareness? Literally or energetically walk away and give your overthinking mind a rest. Frequently, brilliant ideas or answers come from the space between your thoughts, not from the process of analyzing itself. It is in this space that you receive communication from yourself. This is a phenomenon described in various ways by past and present scientists, inventors, poets, writers, artists, and leaders doing beneficial work in the world, including Albert Einstein. who said, "The intuitive mind is a sacred gift and the rational mind is a faithful servant. We have created a society that honors the servant and has forgotten the gift." And, "The only real valuable thing is intuition."

Without space, there can be no collaboration between your intellect and your intuitive awareness. Have you ever noticed that as your intuition, analyzer, and intellect are all playing nicely together, the self-critical, overthinking mind jumps in to squash the whole endeavor? It's like the intellect seems to hijack intuition right when it's getting its groove on. The following story will illuminate the process.

Imagine you're sitting on a boulder along a forest trail, or daydreaming on your couch, but in your mind, you're quietly mapping out an incredible plot for a novel or a groundbreaking idea for renewable energy that will improve the environment. You are primed with intellectual training in your area of expertise, your analyzer is clear, fresh, and spacious today, and the puzzle pieces are moving into place to manifest your vision.

Another excellent idea lands and creative intuition is alive and well! Who cares where it came from, don't analyze that part! Let go of the intellect's constant interruptions and stay in the flow of your awareness. It's a great idea, so go with it; there is plenty of time to edit later! You *know* this is the correct first step. Later you will follow up in the physical world in ways that will move you out of this pure idea realm and put things into action.

Oops. Your intellect-analyzer team interjects self-critical thoughts following this guidance. Intellect questions, "Are you sure you're capable enough to know what you're doing?" "Do you have time or other important resources to make this happen?"

Bam. As soon as you start to intellectualize and overthink your initial flow of ideas, you step outside of your intuitive knowing. Second-guessing, doubting, overthinking, and worrying are often the result of expecting your intellect to do a job it simply is not capable of performing without the support of your inner guidance. If you don't stay conscious of what is happening, you can identify with all the bookmarked pictures gaining momentum in your mind. If you get distracted with overthinking, you will shut down your creative orchestration like an "off" switch.

There goes your enthusiasm, too, and without the quality (vibrational frequency) of enthusiasm or appreciation, it's hard to keep a creative project going. This is where your inner sense of humor, self-appreciation, or ability to be neutral to your critical feelings can get you quickly back on track. These qualities will give you the space to pause and decide what your response will be. You can move again into the space between thoughts and reenter your creative flow.

Sometimes, returning to inner knowing after self-critical thinking requires a force of inner courage or a *Hello* to your bright presence. Courageously laugh it off and keep developing your ideas or visions, despite the self-critical voice in your head. The overthinking mind thinks it can win if it thinks enough. Now you know differently.

Come Home to Your Intuition

Experience and repetition help you build intuitive trust. With practice, you will come to recognize when you are identifying with your intellect and when you are tuned in to your intuition. The most beneficial relationship is when intuitive knowing and intellect are functioning collaboratively, with your conscious awareness leading the way.

By the way, collaboration doesn't mean living in an intuitive space all the time. For example, imagine again sitting on that boulder in the woods where you have created a pause or space to receive an inner message or idea. Then you apply your intellect by editing, or by working with your hands to engineer a prototype. During that same day, you could receive more intuitive guidance for your next steps, and so on.

> *Your intuition gives you what you need to know, when you need to know it!*

Be sure to give it space and don't critically hijack the message or information you receive. The following is a personal tale that describes the beauty of being at home with your intuition. It also illuminates the downfall of intellectualizing your intuitive knowing.

The Shell Story

I walked on a remote South Pacific beach. The washed-up shells were beautiful, and I picked them up to examine their colors and shapes. Many of the shells housed hermit crabs, some big as golf balls, while other shells lay empty. I waded into the clear, calm water, up to my shins, where there were more shells. Looking into the water, I spotted a completely unique shell and reached toward it. Immediately, my intuitive knowing messaged me, *Don't pick up that shell. It's dangerous.*

I paused and removed my hand from the water but kept my eyes on the shell. I'd never seen a shell like this and was excited to find it. I really wanted to see if it was empty, so I could add it to my collection. Again, I thought about picking it up. *Don't touch. I'm dangerous*, was the next intuitive message that came to me. As I pondered this, I had a seemingly rational thought from my intellect, which said, *That shell is probably not dangerous. There are hermit crabs inhabiting many varieties of shells on this beach. That's just a hermit crab trying to protect itself by sending out a warning, a vibe, that it's dangerous.* After all, as everyone knows, lots of small creatures disguise themselves for protection, like the viceroy butterfly for example.

Nonetheless, instead of picking it up, I walked away in search of shells that were high up on the beach, dried out. I always follow my intuitive downloads, even when I don't know precisely why. In my continual experience collecting intuitive data all these years, the proof relating to my intuitive choices always becomes very clear, anywhere from five minutes to five years later!

Later that day, I was sitting with the family who owned the place where we were staying. On the nearby table was the same type of shell as the one I'd seen that day.

Unprompted, their young daughter pointed to the shell and said, "That shell right there is empty, but if you ever see this shell in the water, don't risk picking it up! It's deadly. The inhabitant of that shell can dart out and prick you, and the poison can kill you very quickly."

I was momentarily stunned and greatly humbled by my lack of information about South Pacific marine life. Mostly though, I was deeply grateful for my relationship with my intuition, and for the trust and respect I'd given it all these years. "Thank you," I told the girl, "That's really, really good to know!" Note to self!

As I reflected on that day with the shell, I saw how the intellect-based thought I'd had, *It was probably only a hermit crab inhabiting the shell and "vibing" me*, presented a logical explanation since the beach was crawling with hermit crabs housed in a variety of shells. It was based on a pretty good assumption, yet it was profoundly flawed information for that specific situation in that moment and location.

Following direct intuitive guidance, our intellect often interjects a critical thought. Intellect can hijack intuition like an authority who thinks they know more. The intuitive guidance gives a simple message, and then our intellect second-guesses or tries to add a choice that increases complexity. Our intellect isn't capable of recognizing that our intuitive knowing can be that immediate, clear, and correct.

Intellect Presents as the Expert

Another example is one time when I was on a busy road, and I needed to stop for gas. I could see several gas stations ahead of me, so I logically chose the first one because it was closest and there were no cars blocking the pump. Right away my inner guidance gently said, *Don't stop there, go to the next gas station.* Instead of following my inner knowing, I let my intellect hijack this succinct message with a logical thought that countered, saying, *Why would there be anything wrong with this gas station? You're imagining things.* Yes! Actually, I was imagining things! A couple of minutes later, I got an answer to my why question. The pump malfunctioned, and gas squirted out all over my hands. Luckily it didn't get on my clothes. Hanging up the pump, I went into the store to let them know what happened. I asked where the bathroom was so I could wash off my hands, but they said they didn't have a public bathroom. Absurdly, I had to purchase a bottle of water just to rinse my hands. By then, my well-developed sense of humor had kicked in, and I was laughing it off instead of feeling resentful. Resentment has a way of replaying emotions which tie up your energy. Yet I was also thinking, *Hello! Humorous note to self: It's not rocket science, follow your intuitive guidance!*

Collect Your Own Intuitive Data

Following your intuitive knowing on a daily basis doesn't need to be dramatic like my shell story. Whether we are aware of it or not, much of everyday existence revolves around making simple intuitive choices. Like what happened at the gas station, simple intuitive choices such as where to pump your gas, where to apply for a new job, or when to text or call a friend, can result in beneficial outcomes and aligned timing. It's possible to save yourself an enormous amount of energy, time, and stress when you're consciously tuned in to your work, communication, responsibilities, and projects. Even exercise, shopping, or vacation have intuitive options. Collecting your own inner data about your day-to-day experiences is a fun way to build trust with yourself.

Consider a situation in the past when your timing was incredibly aligned with solving a challenging problem or situation, or bypassing a hot mess that you didn't need to get caught up in. This might have looked like meeting the right person exactly when you needed them, finding what you were looking for, or coming up with a great idea. Observe what this spacious orchestration is like, and then compare this experience with a time when things got temporarily stuck, or felt full of effort, overwhelm, stress, or detours.

When everything went smoothly, recall if you were able to give some space between your thoughts, a pause of presence that helped you receive solutions, support, ideas, or a clear repetitive knowing. Set your sights on what it was like when it worked well, and also discern what happened when you moved out of that divine orchestration. Did your intellect overwhelm your gentle intuitive knowing, like a loud cell phone talker in a quiet café?

Building an intuitive relationship with yourself involves practice. Make a conscious decision for this to be a joyful and humorous journey of self-discovery where you don't always have to get it right the first time. This is not a school or professional test, rather it's a time for you to become more present to what outcomes are available in every changing moment of your busy day. The experience is like looking at something that's always been there but seeing it in a new light or with new appreciation. You are giving yourself permission to navigate more freely in the world.

Intuitive Tools

Activity 1
Lower the Analyzer's Volume and Give Yourself a Pause

You wear a multitude of hats every day, and each role requires different approaches using your creativity, communication, intellect, and intuition. If you plow through the day without a pause to differentiate your changing roles, your analyzer can unconsciously run without clarity of intentions or goals. This activity will help you develop a more conscious, intuitive relationship with the analyzing mind, to help you pause throughout your day between thoughts, feelings, projects, roles, or work and home life. Manage your analyzer and become the conscious director of a useful tool with many benefits, like getting more done while having more fun or sleeping with fewer interruptions throughout the night or gaining clarity and conscious choice throughout your day.

Directions

1. Sit comfortably in a chair with both feet on the floor.
2. Give yourself three deep, conscious breaths.
3. Say *Hello* to your body and your bright soul presence.
4. Give yourself permission to experience your intuition in action in this moment.
5. Imagine your day's transitions, moving from project to project or role to role. Going from home to work, or from work to pick up your child and then to the store before heading home, or returning a ton of work emails and calls then shifting gears to be fully present to your spouse or friend. Witness all the thoughts that arise when thinking about these events. Say *Hello* to your analytical, overthinking mind!
6. Pause to greet your analyzer warmly, like a valued friend.
7. Observe the condition of your analyzing mind. Is it chattering loudly, like it has had too much espresso? Is it dominating your space by pushing you along, when you'd actually like a peaceful pause? Is it in a state of effort to solve everyone's problems right now, instantly, and to be responsible for everything?
8. Quiet your analyzer by asking it to turn down the volume or intensity level to a more comfortable, optimized, balanced level for you in the present moment.

9. Quiet your analyzer by placing its chattering thoughts, outer directives, or images into bubbles (or roses), that you can disintegrate in an instant (Activity 1, Chapter 2.).
10. Reset your energy with the Golden Sun activity (Activity 1, Chapter 1).
11. Say *Hello* again to your analyzing mind. Think of the day's events again. Notice if your thoughts or feelings have changed, and in what way. Is there a new quality of energy to them? Do you experience less stress or effort, more inner trust, space, balance, calm, peace, or clarity to refine or redefine which hats you wish to wear today?
12. Create a pause in your transitions. For example, do this activity before you get out of the car, and note any differences as you walk through the door to your job or back home at the end of your day. During your day, notice when overly critical, fix-it-now, or other unwanted thoughts arise. You can do this activity while sitting at your desk, in the bathroom or hall, during meditation, on a walk, while cooking dinner or eating lunch, or immediately before bed to improve sleep quality—anywhere and anytime you need it.

Activity 2
The Rose: Is This My Problem to Solve?

An undirected analyzer often fills the mind with other people's problems, and then places responsibility for solutions upon your shoulders. It is easy to absorb another's pain, anxiety, or worries as your own, without knowing it. When you carry someone else's energy, you create problems that have no solutions because these problems are not yours to solve. They belong to someone else. Once you stop spending so much energy trying to solve problems that are not yours, you are free to focus on your own clarity and personal solutions. As a result, you can also discern the most effective ways to support others and apply your abilities to improve the world around you. It's a win-win! This activity provides an intuitive tool to help you to distinguish between your own and others' energy. This intuitive tool works best when you are in a space of qualities such as appreciation, laughter, joy, imagination, creativity, or intuitive curiosity, not solely in your... intellect (yup, you guessed it!).

Directions

1. Sit comfortably with both feet on the floor and give yourself three conscious breaths.
2. Give yourself permission to experience your intuition in action in this moment.
3. Greet yourself as the bright presence you are by validating your light and your power within. Say *Hello* to yourself! Quiet your analyzer by asking it to turn down the volume or intensity level to an optimized, balanced level for you in the present moment.
4. Think of a problem you've been trying to solve.
5. Envision the image of a rose about four feet in front of you.
6. Attach a stem to the rose that instantly grounds it to the earth.
7. Allow your problem to enter the petals of the rose. You may see it as a thought, colors, image, symbol, feeling, frequency of energy, etc.
8. Imagine any energy that does not belong to you drains into the earth through the stem of the rose. Don't think it through or try to figure out what is or is not yours with your intellect.
9. Watch what happens to the rose. If the rose shrivels, disappears, melts, or crinkles, know that this is not your problem to solve. If you receive this result, you are finished with this exercise and can fill with golden suns.
10. If the rose stays fully intact, or only partially disappears or shrivels, it is at least partly your problem to solve.
11. What percentage of the rose remains intact? Perhaps it's only 25 percent intact. This is the percentage of the problem that is yours to solve. Very little of it might be yours. Collaboration may be required to get to an effective resolution.
12. Visualize a golden sun above the remaining part of the rose.

13. Within that golden sun, postulate or welcome a positive solution to your problem (that you know, or don't yet know, but you imagine is possible).
14. Fill the rose with the golden sun containing that solution.
15. Now imagine there's a place in your body or energy field that supports the solution. Let your golden light-filled rose fill that space within or around you.
16. See, know, or feel what solution the rose shows you. Be open to this knowing. It is your choice to act upon this new knowledge. Intend that your next steps manifest with divine timing for the highest good of all.

Activity 3
The Filter Rose

This is another way you can apply the visualization of a rose. Since we absorb energy (emotions, thoughts, opinions, pictures, etc.) from the world around us, this rose visualization is an intuitive tool that gives you more space from energy (outside of you) that is not yours.

Directions

1. Sit comfortably with both feet on the floor and give yourself three conscious breaths.
2. Give yourself permission to experience your intuition in action in this moment.
3. Greet yourself as the bright presence you are by validating your light and your power within. Say *Hello* to yourself! Quiet your analyzer by asking it to turn down the volume or intensity level to an optimized, balanced level for you in the present moment.
4. Imagine a rose that is three or four feet in front of you, with a stem that goes into the earth.
5. Allow this rose to represent your own true energy signature in present time as a color or colors. You can also visualize the quality of the petals, a brightness or other characteristics that represent your authentic energy.

6. As you go about your normal day, intend for this rose to absorb and filter any energy that might otherwise end up in your space.
7. Occasionally during your day, explode your filter rose and imagine a new one with a stem that goes into the earth. Each time you create a fresh filter rose, it may look different (colors or other qualities) because your energy is always changing.
8. Create a new filter rose every morning before you start your day, and again at the end of your day.
9. Observe the way this rose is intended to give you more neutrality, peace, and space to be. Let this rose remind you that you can have your own space, even while surrounded by lots of other people and energy from the world around you.

Chapter Four
Grounding: A Present and Healing Relationship with Your Body

Grounded Energy

Like an electric fence, a current of energy flows through your body. I enjoy this image because I grew up hurdling electric fences like a track and field star to get places quickly on our farm. An electric fence has ground rods which provide an electrical path to safely discharge excess energy into the ground so the system doesn't malfunction when struck by lightning, for example. Just as a ground rod establishes a connection with the earth, you can apply your intuitive awareness to consciously ground yourself through a practice of creative visualization.

> *You are a generator of energy—a creative power energizer!*

Grounding helps you safely and efficiently discharge excess energy that is not yours. The earth, upon which you stand, literally has zero electrical potential. Grounding supports you to run your normal energies with continuous ease.

Let's say a tree branch falls on the electric fence. The current along the fence is weakened until the debris is cleared. When lightning strikes, the electrical energizer system might even blow a circuit. What is the debris in *your* life that weakens your system? Have you occasionally (or more than occasionally) blown a circuit? Everyone's currents can be disrupted or weakened from energy obstructions.

The practice of grounding into the earth allows you to discharge absorbed energy and/or release the debris from your space that you unconsciously collected. From this space, suddenly there is room for a flow that provides soul-body team unity. Grounding is a conscious, creative, and imaginative practice of awareness in your mind that also lets you communicate in present time with your body, so you are in sync.

When your energy flow is unobstructed, you create more space to heal. When your energy is blocked, you are more likely to get stuck on unwanted emotions which destabilize your inner power. Once you experience being grounded, it's easier to recognize when your energy is blocked, then reboot and stabilize through grounding. For instance, have you ever been injured or sick, and then blamed yourself for this situation? Talk about adding insult to injury! Instead, this is a great time to release that emotional debris and say *Hello* to grounding your body, which gives it greater power to heal and feel safe.

Grounding through the Body

Grounding is the key to becoming more present to your experiences in every changing moment of your life. Your body is the vessel through which you express your bright presence, which includes your intellect and senses. Grounding is the way you anchor and embody your soul presence. If you look in the mirror, your eyes look brighter when you're grounded. This is because you're letting the bright power of your soul presence shine. Your body loves to be grounded; even your voice range changes when you are grounded. Grounding also increases your balance, spatial awareness, situational awareness while driving, and reaction time, giving you the space to discern when to calmly respond, or when to react in times of danger. It's an aware and observant state of mind to be in while walking in a city, crowded place, or while on your cell phone. When grounded, it's easier to hold your space in situations where you feel less sure of yourself.

> *An experience gained through practiced awareness, grounding is a way of being in a direct and present relationship with your body.*

The stability of grounding helps you step out of survival-thinking mode, mentally or emotionally. A grounded mind shifts attention from trying to fix things in areas where you have little control (the hamster wheel) and creates stability where you stand firmly in your areas of knowledge. A grounded person is able to listen more fully and express more clearly from their bright presence.

Being disengaged from your body destabilizes the energy of your whole physical system. This can cause various levels of anxiety or stress running with a subtle buzz in the background of your mind. This is just one way of experiencing ungroundedness. When you are in an ungrounded state, you aren't able to manage your energy. Grounding is an energy processor. When you are grounded, it's as if you are saying to your body, *Okay, we've got this, we can do this, together!*

On the broadest levels, grounding creates a foundation for you to show up and put your ideas into focused action and expression, and not get so easily knocked down by the inevitable storms. Becoming grounded creates the safety you require to open your awareness and heart to a wider lens on the world. It can even help you find the divine comedy in the midst of life's dramas.

Grounding Is Innate, Not Intellectual

Being grounded is totally optional for the intellect. If the intellect is dominating your space, and you are ungrounded, you disengage from your body. Even while disconnected from your body awareness, the intellect can still run at 100 percent, performing learned technical or other functional skills. This is known as living in your head and is a different experience than living in a grounded state. In this state, it can be a challenge to manage your energy effectively or efficiently. Significant trade-offs or imbalances come with living this way.

In our culture, these practices aren't taught alongside math and reading skills. Being grounded is innately familiar, and once it's validated it can become a conscious relationship between soul and body presence. Grounding *is* something you need to practice, to access your state of embodied awareness and build this intuitive relationship. It helps to make a conscious decision to practice this every day. The outcome? Despite the frenzied world around you, inside you will find more peace and calm impacting every aspect of your day.

When you approach life in a more grounded way, you are also consciously deciding to show up and be engaged in your personal development, actions, observations, and feelings. Not everyone seeks this path, although it seems the easier way to live in this wild and unpredictable world. Grounding is an innate support system for you, and for all of us.

Because our culture has lost touch with this knowledge, grounding is not often consciously applied in our everyday lives. As a result, many people may struggle with effective ways of grounding. Grounding happens naturally through exercise and is supported with adequate sleep and healthful food that includes protein. Animals are a grounding presence, inviting us to match them. The natural world also invites us to become grounded, whether it's a city park or a vast wilderness.

You can also be rested but ungrounded, ungrounded while exercising (resulting in an injury), or you may unconsciously overeat as a way to *try* to ground yourself. Some unknowingly seek out extreme sports because the adrenaline rush (a bodily survival state) will bring an ungrounded person temporarily back to their body. Some may overuse alcohol or drugs to cope with feelings of ungroundedness, yet these activities cause ungroundedness. Each day brings different ungrounding factors. You can be grounded anytime, anywhere, and you don't need to seek it outside of yourself. Your goal is to practice creating a grounded relationship with your body and senses.

Ungrounded Journeys: No Space to Respond Intuitively

When there is no pause between thoughts, your intuition has no space to respond from your deep well of wisdom. The ungrounded mind follows a rapid run of associative bookmarked images, like a bird flitting from tree to tree. On these journeys, you naturally hover away from your body, disconnected or unaware. You become a bit numb to what's going on within and around you.

The following are examples of these ungrounded journeys where your intellect is still working while other parts of you have "left the building." Have you ever driven a route every day, and during that drive, you suddenly realize you've been driving for fifteen minutes and don't remember experiencing the drive itself? Or have you ever been in a meeting or at a party, and missed a whole chunk of conversation or information because you spaced out? If the answer is *yes*, you're in good company. In over a thousand classes where I've taught grounding, everyone has experienced this phenomenon in their daily lives!

Many people describe everyday experiences of viewing themselves out of their bodies, watching what is happening, but unable to fully interact or engage. This can occur when you're under stress, during a trauma, when you feel ashamed, judged, scared, uncertain, angry, sad, super excited (a game-show winner), bored (a tired teen in health class), or when someone is pressuring you from their agenda (well-meaning or not). Without grounding, it's easier for energy to impact your mental and emotional well-being. Sometimes being ungrounded (in the clouds) can be a happy place, too, a place of daydreaming or fantasy, but that's not really where we are meant to live and do our most orchestrated work.

One day I was unable to work in my private office, so I sat in a coffee shop getting some important work completed on a deadline. A dog sitting next to me kept jumping up and barking whenever another dog came in. Although I love dogs, I got distracted trying to figure out why someone would bring their sweet dog to a quiet coffee shop when it couldn't stop barking at other dogs.

This linked to my next bookmarked picture, where I wondered why the owners of the coffee shop didn't suggest that a barking dog wasn't appropriate for such a space. *Should I say something?* I kept thinking. No, I was raised by a British mother, and, like a Monty Python skit, British people are trained not to complain, even when their arm is falling off. (Cue Monty Python images!)

My mind next traveled to our dog at home who enjoys chasing birdseed-stealing squirrels off our front porch, even though he never catches them. This reminded me of my husband. I then sent him a text with a unicorn blowing him a kiss, which made me feel like I'm in eighth grade. In this ungrounded reverie, I had a moment of gratitude that I am no longer in middle school but can still act like it sometimes. Then I thought about my daughter's social plans this upcoming weekend, and the complex transportation logistics involved since I would be her chauffeur. And on and on. Sound familiar?

As humans, we all do this, it's only a matter of how often and its impact upon our daily lives. When we become aware of being ungrounded, it simply gives us the opportunity to come back to a grounded place again.

> *You (unintentionally) unground, you notice, you reground. The more that practice occurs, the more you become grounded.*

A Space to Respond from Inner Power

A response begins with a momentary pause, a space, an offering. It's a giving energy, balanced as active and receptive. When you ground, you come back into your body, stabilizing your energy to access more inner resources, such as your inner guidance. Each time you validate or say *Hello* to your intuitive awareness, you expand the context in which you see yourself. Immediately, this opens space to see others in a new light, rather than through the old pictures absorbed from your past experiences. Grounding helps you respond to life with more space, adaptability, and creative mobility.

As a word, *grounded* sometimes means down to earth, honest, or plainspoken. Yet, that's like reading only the outside cover of a book. Grounding is a sustainable, embodied, practical practice that is not about your personality type, job, or lifestyle preferences.

You don't have to take your shoes off and sink your toes into the dirt (though that's nice too). The real core of grounding lies inside you, as creative power. You can access it anytime, anywhere, and the more you practice, the more available it becomes. In this way, you might say that grounding is an act of rebellion since it makes it harder to be controlled by outside forces. When you own your space, you hold your space. Grounding creates safety for you to know that you have autonomous ownership of your body, which liberates you to be more aware of your inner freedom. When you live your life from a grounded presence, you are the spiritual and emotional director of your life, and you have easier access to your own answers. This kind of autonomy is an essential ingredient to unify and collaborate with others.

> *An individual or group of people who are in charge of their own lives through grounding is a powerful foundation for conscious expression and positive action.*

Mia's Story: Refresh and Reset Energy through Grounding

Mia was a highly skilled and compassionate mental health therapist, with a busy work and family life. At the end of each day, she enjoyed wine with dinner. She began a new health routine and decided to have one glass of wine two times per week, instead of every night. As soon as she made that change, she felt irritated at her partner and three teens, all of whom she adored! It was so hard to deny herself that glass of wine to relax her body and switch off the subtle background energy of analyzing her patients long after leaving the office.

She didn't like this feeling of needing the wine medicinally. The emotional energy of her patients that was occupying her space translated into annoyance at her family. Mia had a sinking feeling that she wasn't clearing out their emotional energy; she was just numbing it down. She had always been aware that it was important to let go of the workday, yet she'd never been taught an effective way to do that.

Her coping skill had always been to make herself stop thinking about work, yet that wasn't really doing the trick for her anymore. She was feeling guilty and grumpy simultaneously, yet couldn't talk herself out of feeling that way. She hadn't yet realized that she was matching the energy of her patients, and this was causing her to become ungrounded. In an ungrounded state, she had less access to her inner resources.

Mia's friend Paul was a doctor with a similar experience. He shared with Mia that one day, while a patient was talking to him, Paul admitted to himself that he was often not present and hearing what the patient was saying. Paul realized that he was unconsciously absorbing the suffering of his patients, precisely because he cared deeply about everyone's well-being. In an effort to handle the energy, he compartmentalized it. All of this was making it harder for Paul to be a compassionate listener, a quality he personally valued.

Transitioning from work to home was not always easy. Work energy caused Paul quiet levels of grief that he brought home every day. When he got home, he had a desire to retreat as he felt like he did not have enough space for himself to be compassionate to his, his patients', and his spouse's needs. To manage everyone's different needs, he had to use varied creative approaches. In an attempt to reboot from work energy, he exercised for several hours a day. Although his body became stronger physically, it wasn't healing his emotional body. The many years of intellectual training never clued him in on what he most needed so that he could live a balanced and healthy life. It's ironic because he loved to help people get healthy. Luckily, even though somewhere along the way it had been left in a dark room, he did have a sense of humor. Time to turn on the light!

Paul's goal was to love his job *and* not burn out. So, he learned how to ground himself via creative visualizations. He practiced before work and during the day as soon as he noticed that he was mentally or emotionally checking out. *Hello* grounding! Grounding visualization provided Paul the stability and space to be present and release energy on the go during his chaotic day. Once he began this practice, he barely had to think about it!

Soon after this conversation with Paul, Mia learned to ground herself while at work. At the end of her workday, she refreshed her grounding, cleared out her space, and reset her energy before she drove home to greet her family. By the time she walked in the door, she felt more enthusiastic about changing gears into family and social time. She literally felt like she had more energy, but it really was the quality of energy that was different for her. Mia was no longer compelled to medicate with wine, so when she drank it two times a week, she enjoyed it more.

Instead of feeling sharp-edged during her transition from work to home, Mia felt inner warmth toward herself that reflected outward. She felt irritated far less often, and when she did have an occasional rough day, she was more straightforward about letting her family know that she just needed some space. For the first time, she didn't feel guilty for not being perfect; this was so freeing! Mia's practice of grounding was helping her to be more intuitive, so when feelings surfaced, she could make conscious what had been unconscious.

Her spouse and teens commented on her changed energy, saying, "You seem happier and more relaxed. Did you go to the spa recently?"

"Yes," she told them. "I went to the energy spa."

Avery's Grounding Story

Avery discovered grounding, which, in turn, enhanced her intuition. She had great ideas to share with the start-up company where she worked. Yet whenever Avery attended large meetings, she could not succinctly express those ideas in a way that could be readily heard or understood. Instead, Avery would share her ideas in more detail with a colleague, privately. Sometimes a colleague would even bring up her idea with others, and get the credit for it. Avery felt unseen and undervalued.

Avery had always been aware of being sensitive and insightful about what was going on with people around her. In school, she had often known the answers to questions before looking them up. Teachers sometimes wondered how she just *knew* the answer. This carried over into Avery's dynamic ideas for work, but she struggled to articulate them while in large groups.

One day, knowing there had to be resources that would somehow support her, Avery registered for a class to learn intuitive tools. She learned how to ground. After a few months of practicing on the go at work, something changed on a subtle yet powerful level. At big meetings, Avery would consciously ground, then share from her notes the ideas she had jotted down. She was then able to clearly recognize what caused her to check out of her grounded awareness previously. Because she became overwhelmed when everyone's attention (as energy) was on her, as soon as she felt it, she would unintentionally unground. This made it difficult for her to communicate what she had to share.

She learned that she could reclaim ownership of her body and space and feel safe while in the spotlight. She was no longer going to miss valuable opportunities to share her ideas at meetings. Avery was deeply happy to finally be heard and seen for the value she brought to the workplace. An added bonus was that she also received a raise.

Survival Thinking: An Ungrounded State

As you grow up, you develop coping mechanisms that allow you to get by or get through your tasks, roles, jobs, and conversations. When the intellectual mind is solely running the show, it will create and follow patterns based on these coping mechanisms, on repeat. In this busy world, you are expected to keep up or compete at a frantic pace. All of these factors merge into a kind of constant comparison, an overthinking pace that can put a person into survival thinking.

Survival thinking is an ungrounded state of mind that says, I will never have or be enough. This can send you scrambling after more things like affection, people, money, responsibilities, or stuff. Popular people can sometimes be motivated to have as many friends or followers as possible because they equate approval with survival. A person could have ten million dollars, and still feel like they are in survival mode. This ungrounded, lack mentality is embedded into our culture.

> **Survival thinking creates stress.**

Survival thinking also creates reactivity. Reactivity does not provide you with the space to pause, access your creative intuition, and choose the wisest path forward in any decision. Living in survival thinking is completely different from living in a true physical survival situation, where your ability to react may be very important!

Survival thinking closes down your most valuable levels of creativity, imagination, energy, and adaptability. When you can't access your intuitive creativity, you can end up with ungrounding survival thoughts like feelings of disempowerment, bookmarked "movies" in your mind, set on quiet background levels of guilt, isolation, resentment, anxiety, frustrations, or anger.

Since everyone is intuitive, if a person combines ungrounded survival thinking from a "taking" space of energy, with unconscious intuition, they can veer off course. For example, consider the head of a corporation who does not have the interests of the natural environment in mind or is selling a product that's harmful to humans or animals, or maybe it's a financial adviser who has their own best interests in mind rather than their client's financial well-being.

At the same time, there are people founding companies who are unconsciously intuitively creating positive outcomes. Because of their energy, they are creating in an enormously beneficial way for the highest good. A good example would be generating from a giving space rather than a taking space, thereby creating from wholeness, versus from… well, "half-ness." Being in an energy space of "givingness" heals the planet and humanity!

> *By the way, givingness isn't giving it all away; it's a reciprocal space of energy, a win-win for all involved.*

Grounded awareness transforms survival thinking. It helps you to become present to whatever resources are available or imaginable.

You can also become ungrounded when you keep trying to solve or fix things out of your control. When you intuitively distinguish what you can control, it enables you to embody a grounded energy of abundance, creativity, collaboration, and inner freedom. Grounding helps navigate the busy, distracted, uncertain world in which we live.

You build new neuronal responses when you transform survival thinking into grounded awareness. These new responses cycle into more feelings of grounded well-being over time. In this way, grounding guides you back into your power. A grounded body has freedom to access soul and body presence, creative power, wisdom, authentic communication, and humor.

Boo! Are You Grounded?

There's a way to quickly tell whether you are grounded or not. Note that you may be more or less grounded on different days depending on the circumstances. As an adult, have you ever had someone playfully sneak up on you, to jump out and say boo? My daughter used to do that to me all the time. Whether you enjoy that or not, when you're grounded, it's unlikely that you'll jump or be too upset when that happens.

If you do react with a jump or a scream, or feel your heart race, the gift of that experience is direct feedback that you are out of your body. The scare sharply brings you back! Perhaps it's an opportunity to see that you were stressing about the future or were lost in the past. Maybe you were having a super fun time in your unlimited imagination, but in a disembodied way.

Your body doesn't really enjoy being scared or surprised. Without a loving, present guide (you!), your body can't always make sense of what's happening. The shock wakes you up to return to being the captain of your own ship.

> **When you become aware that you are not grounded, and then intentionally ground yourself, you calm your nervous system and relax back into your creative, intuitive spaciousness.**

Give yourself a compassionate and loving pause to become grounded in the present moment when you stub your toe on the furniture, bump your head on the car door, space out while driving or at a meeting, or leave a pan cooking on the stove for too long. Don't waste time judging yourself; just reground, and move on.

Grounding Dreams Through the Earth

Because your ability to ground yourself is available and present at all times, you need not look too far to find your teammate for grounding: the earth. You are made of both the earth and cosmos. The earth itself has a calming, grounding effect. As your imagination reaches into the cosmos for possibilities and solutions, the earth helps you anchor into those possibilities. As you walk this landscape, consciously choosing to be grounded to the earth is a healing for all.

Animals have a lot to teach us about grounding and being present because it's not a thinking thing, it's a state of beingness. Horses, dogs, and other animals live in this state.

When I was a child, growing up on hundreds of acres of organic, regenerative farmland, I had a lot of freedom. I lived in a vibrant inner world of active imagination and awareness, yet I was often ungrounded. I recall one time spacing out and walking directly into our electric fence. It zapped me right across the forehead, like some kind of rude but comical awakening: *Hello! Come on back to earth, daydreamer!*

Back then I traveled to far off places, imagining creating a place in the world where I could help others and share my creativity, insights, and observations in beneficial ways. Had I been aware of how to ground myself, I would have been both physically and intuitively aware of the fence well before I hit it. Although I didn't know specific grounding tools, I found my grounding sanctuary amid the middle of a huge sheep flock in the field. Had I learned that I could be like a tree with roots deep in the ground, I may have started out with a deeper awareness that I could be present *and* imaginative, at the same time. That's what I call soul-body teamwork! Once I began to consciously practice grounding because of my extreme out-of-body experience when I was four, it was easy for me to recognize that being out of my body was on a wide spectrum of experience and awareness, and being in my body was incredibly innate.

Bringing It All Together: Reground and Reboot

If I'm stressed about a problem without a clear solution, I consider all my choices. One choice is to let the energy of my mental chatter fall like debris into my energy flow. This chatter feels like I'm moving fast in five opposing directions and burning up a lot of my precious time. Although one of those directions might be part of the solution, it's very hard to intuitively discern this until I stop overthinking.

When we are feeling ungrounded, we might be unaware that bookmarked pictures are running our show. We can find ourselves temporarily overriding, resisting, or becoming some of that energy. When this happens, people having a hard time will sometimes say, "I can't even think straight right now." Or they might tell themselves they are fine, but not really feel that way.

Whenever I space out into the land of overthinking, overanalyzing, and emotional-survival autopilot, I ground myself. When you create a conscious pause, space, or moment to stop being on overdrive, your body can settle down and access a doorway to your creative, intuitive solutions. Meditation and grounding can support each other to bring you into the present moment. Many busy people who meditate describe how they can't sustain their meditation practice longer than a specific number of minutes even though they'd like to increase it. Bringing grounding into a meditation practice allows you to manage the distraction energy that would otherwise eject you from your space.

If in your space your energy has nowhere to ground, you have less space "to be." In the same way, metaphorically speaking, you can't step into a room that is filled to the brim with stuff. But if you're not aware that your room is full because the "stuff" is invisible to you, you still react to it.

> **When you feel constricted, stressed, under pressure, or aggravated, you can ground yourself, and create space for all of you, the bright soul presence you are.**

As you practice being grounded during meditation, it becomes easier to let go of over-reviewing past conversations from your day. Your inner wisdom can reset your thoughts or feelings, rather than allowing energy collected during your day to dictate your experience or feelings. This quickly breaks the cycle of following bookmarked picture patterns, brings you back into your body, and realigns you with your purpose.

> **In a grounded, creative flow, I am more open to receiving inner questions and answers that bring greater clarity. Often, I receive information for the next few steps forward.**

Finally, imagine your chatter as extraneous baggage. Don't negotiate with the chatter because it creates effort, resistance, or inner pushback. Instead, imagine checking that chatter the way you would check a bag at an airport. By doing so, it supports your grounding.

When you practice slowing down and find the pauses between your thoughts, you will be much more present to resources that are available. Since grounding is an innate aspect of your soul and body relationship, it also connects you more deeply with all aspects of life.

Intuitive Tools

Activity 1
Grounding Cord Basics: Let Your Energy Flow

You have the power to ground yourself and move on to more productive, creative, intuitive, and joyful experiences. Grounding stabilizes you on spiritual, physical, emotional, and mental levels. It allows you to release energy like fear or stress and gives you greater conscious ownership of your creative power.

In this activity, you will practice the basics of grounding to validate your bright presence, express more aspects of yourself, and experience daily empowered ownership of your body. Grounding is an inside job. Make a conscious decision to practice grounding every day, during meditation and definitely while on the go. An added bonus: You'll observe, listen, and share more often.

Directions

1. Sit in a chair with your feet on the floor. Give yourself three conscious breaths.
2. Thank your amazing body by joyfully appreciating all the ways it supports you.
3. Greet yourself as the soul presence you are by validating your bright light and your power within. Say *Hello* to yourself! Quiet your analyzer by asking it to turn down the volume or intensity level to an optimized, balanced level for you in the present moment.
4. Validate that you are centered behind your eyes in your neutral awareness.
5. Give yourself 100 percent permission to imagine. And have fun!
6. Imagine a grounding cord that you visualize as a thick, stable trunk of a tree, as wide as your hips (or wider), that reaches all the way down from the tip of your tailbone to the center of the earth (approximately 4,000 miles). Envision this tree trunk as well-anchored, so nothing can unground you. If you're sitting, you might imagine sitting on this tree trunk. If you stand, walk, or lie down, picture this cord equally anchored as when you are in a sitting position.
7. Imagine your tree trunk is conductive, with an energetic flow that discharges energy down into the earth. Say *Hello* to your grounded awareness! Validate (or decide) that you are grounded, in your body.

8. Write your name (your energy signature) on your grounding cord. You are the energizer, and grounding lets your energy flow.
9. The energy you release drops to the center of the earth, disperses, and is neutralized. Appreciate the effectiveness of your grounding cord's abilities.
10. Over time, observe if grounding calms your nervous system and brings greater stability or awareness on emotional, spiritual, mental, and physical levels. Discover if you have more space to be, see, know, listen, be present, laugh, and take action!

Activity 2
Collect Intuitive Data on Your Grounded Awareness

Once you experience being grounded and practice it each day, you will consciously know when you are *not* grounded. It is through recognizing when you're *not* grounded that you embody your innate groundedness! In this activity, discover what qualities of thoughts, opinions, emotions, body sensations, situations, settings, or relationships cause you to unground or destabilize.

Increasing awareness of what causes you to unground allows you to reground faster, even while on the go. Recognize those times when you've lost your grounding, then empower yourself and consciously grow, nurture yourself, transform old patterns, and heal. This activity helps you track intuitive data on your groundedness journey so you can mark progress and identify areas for continued growth.

Directions

1. Sit in a chair with your feet on the floor. Give yourself three conscious breaths.
2. Say *Hello* to your amazing body. Say *Hello* to yourself as the bright soul presence you are.
3. Ground yourself. (See activity 1 for more details.) Quiet your analyzer by asking it to turn down the volume or intensity level to an optimized, balanced level for you in the present moment.
4. Validate that you are centered behind your eyes in your neutral awareness.

5. Make a list (written or audio) of any thoughts, feelings, activities, hobbies, body sensations, situations, settings, or relationships that support and lead to feeling grounded in your body.
6. Make a list of any thoughts, emotions, body sensations, situations, settings, opinions, directives, or relationships that generally cause you to temporarily unground, space out, stop observing, or stop listening.
7. Reflect upon what it feels like in both your body and mind to be grounded and ungrounded. What is the quality of that energy?
8. Imagine or visualize three bookmarked pictures, thoughts, emotions, or qualities that unground you and decide to release them into a bubble. Throw that bubble down your grounding cord and allow the energy to be neutralized. Also, you can revisit Activity 1, Chapter 2 and pop some bubbles (or roses).
9. Replenish your space using the Golden Sun activity (Activity 1, Chapter 1). Fill yourself with golden sun life force energy that contains the qualities of groundedness you seek, such as peace, calm, self-love, compassion, stability, joy, confidence, personal power, and appreciation.

Activity 3
Observing Where You Go

Sometimes where your attention goes, you go. When you space out, are bored, stressed, become upset or angry, or are enthralled in something in front of you, you can become ungrounded and disconnected from your body awareness. When you are grounded and centered, you are less likely to go out of your space to observe; you are therefore more intuitive and have body awareness and stronger observational skills to see and be present to what is in your physical surroundings.

Directions

1. Sit in a chair with your feet on the floor. Give yourself three conscious breaths.

Grounding A Present and Healing Relationship with Your Body

2. Thank your amazing body by appreciating all the ways it supports you. Tell your body: You are safe and loved.
3. Greet yourself as the soul presence you are by appreciating your bright light and your power within. Say *Hello* to yourself!
4. Quiet your analyzer by asking it to turn down the volume or intensity level to an optimized, balanced level for you in the present moment.
5. With eyes open, notice an object in front of you, such as a framed picture on the wall, a window, or an electrical outlet. Close your eyes.
6. Decide that when you open your eyes, you will immediately look at whatever you have chosen to observe. Open your eyes.
7. When you opened your eyes, did you go out to view the object? Or did you stay in your own space, centered behind your eyes in your neutral awareness, to view the object?
8. Repeat the exercise but this time: 1) Validate that you are centered behind your eyes in your neutral awareness. This is a space for you to be centered and to observe without going out of your space. 2) Ground yourself before you go through the steps. (Refer to Activity 1 on grounding.)

Notice if you had a different experience once you were grounded and centered behind your eyes in your neutral awareness. Were you more aware of staying in your space? During your daily activities, notice when you leave your space to look versus when you stay grounded and centered. For example, when you stay grounded in your own space while listening, you will remember more of what is said, rather than going out with your attention to look at something that distracts you. If you stay grounded in your space while driving, rather than letting your attention take you out to look, you will have greater situational awareness and not miss a turn or oncoming obstacle in the road as easily. When in various kinds of stressful situations, our inclination may be to go out, but if you stay grounded in your space and centered, you can navigate with more power and awareness.

Chapter Five
Building Everyday Trust with Your Amazing Intuition

Trust the Value of Everyday Intuition

In our culture, we are given silent and spoken messages that anything worth having has to be fought for or done the hard way, that the hard work is proof of its value or better yet *our* value. That's why we are told, *no pain, no gain*. Effort is a quality of intellect which attracts overthinking. Many things in life are hard, that's true, but because the intellect needs to defend its position from every possible angle, we think nothing can be simple, even when it may be.

> *Your intuition just knows. Your inner knowing has nothing to prove. Although it may be repetitive, it is not trying to persuade you or substantiate the advantages of its value. Your intuition is literally defenseless because it does not defend or argue.*

In our culture, it is harder to trust and validate our inner guidance because it has not been officially given a place at the intellect-dominant table. Yet the more you utilize your inner knowing in an everyday way, the more you can apply it and see its fruition. Allowing yourself to be intuitive every day is the fastest way to begin trusting it.

If you only utilize your inner guidance during the most challenging, desperate, or dramatic events of your life, sometimes there's a tendency to discredit the supporting role of intuition when the event is over. Why? Because the intellect reviews the events in past-time and builds a thesis or defense to confirm that the inner knowing is incorrect or a one-shot deal. Since intuition is not invested in defending or proving itself, it will not refute any of that overthinking mind chatter.

Hone your intuitive skills every day, just like you build your intellectual skills. Learn to trust inner guidance as much as you trust your intellect.

Besides our intellectual training, intuition gives us access to some of the most valuable answers we need to navigate in the world as creative beings, professionals, parents, leaders, family members, and global citizens. With clear intuitive discernment, you can catalyze the power of your inner knowing into brilliant ideas for businesses, art projects, communication, or community building. It's time to validate *your* areas of intuitive strength.

The Signs of Intuition

By validating your inner knowing, you befriend your awareness. How can you tell the signs of intuition so you can apply them and build intuitive awareness and trust? I like to make inner guidance fun while integrating it into my daily life. For example, if I'm skiing in the woods and come to a fork in the trail, I ask for clear guidance and follow it. I'm often rewarded with the results like when I spot a few deer or an owl or find a special place to rest in the sunshine. I use my inner knowing in the grocery store while choosing new foods that I haven't yet tried. Intuition also helps me select a new restaurant, locate an open parking spot in a busy area, or choose an interesting new place to visit.

> *With practice, your awareness will cue your intuitive signs and allow you to shift your attention away from the efforts and complexity of the intellectual mind.*

The following are some signs of intuition to get you started:

Simple Versus Complex

When a personal decision, thought, or action seems overly complex, you are overthinking a situation and getting nowhere, and/or you or those around you have a need to verify a particular point of view as right, you are *not* on the pathway of intuition! When a solution or idea seems too simple, easy, or effortless, and you disregard it, but it keeps gently or lovingly circling back to you, that is likely your intuition ringing your doorbell. When you apply your intuitive awareness, it's possible to choose a way that has more ease, which generally feels more rewarding.

Present Time

Present time, grounded observation is a welcome sign of intuition. Past-time repetition is usually typical of the overthinking mind. An example might be when two people have an endless back-and-forth argument. Instead of making choices to create space for new solutions, they rehash the past through intellectual ways of proving something is either right or wrong based on familiar, old, bookmarked patterns. If you notice that you go off track making assumptions about how something is going to go, or why someone dislikes you, give yourself a pause, reset your grounded energy, release some pictures (bubble popping), access your inner knowing and see for yourself in the present.

Judgment of Self or Others

So often our judgments are either totally unconscious, or we identify them and immediately attach a judgment of our judgments. It's like a ten-car pileup of thoughts, bookmarked pictures, and emotions all within the space of a moment. Reboot from this pileup by asking simple inner questions like, *Is this judgment true? Is this even my judgment, or am I buying into whatever low vibrational energy, opinion, or directive that's hanging around?* Having clarity about judgments moves them into consciousness. Intuitive tools help you release judgments (bubble popping). The goal isn't perfection, it's to be more aware of the judgment game and where that ties up your attention and time.

Below-the-Surface Energies

When you see beyond the physical surface and become aware of a deeper, inner quality about a person or place, take notice! This is another illuminating cue. Seeing the truth within yourself opens more space to recognize the truth or true intentions of others. As you become more aware of your intuitive signs and cues, you'll start to realize the reason behind this sudden interest. You might observe that a person has a distinctive, interesting, or dynamic attribute that you'd like to nurture within yourself. Maybe you intuit that person is not trustworthy. Or someone's energy might remind you of your parent, sibling, best friend, or a former great teacher. Likewise, you might recognize that a place you're visiting has an energy that's healing for you, or an energy that you don't like, even if you are not sure why that is.

Intuitive Knowing

Have you ever had supportive or creative ideas and solutions show up out of nowhere while you're experiencing a pause from overthinking, taking a quiet walk, driving, having tea, daydreaming, or even while working? For example, a poem, an invention, new ways to communicate or solve a conflict, or the most aligned path forward in a given situation or place seem to appear out of "nowhere." The idea for this book started with an intuitive knowing and it evolved from there, with many more ideas showing up once I began to write it.

One time, due to a road closure, I was detoured through a completely unfamiliar neighborhood and street. My daughter was seven years old at the time, and suddenly said from the back seat, "Stop right here." I pulled over, wondering what was going on. She said, "Can we go to the playground over there?" The little playground was empty, but she really insisted, so I agreed. Five minutes later, one of her friends showed up at the playground! She just knew. That's intuitive knowing in action, and it's a common occurrence that many people have described.

Another example is when I was at the grocery store choosing a bag of grapes. I reached for a specific bag and my intuitive knowing let me know that I should choose a different one. I didn't know the reason until a few minutes later. My friend was working at the checkout, and when she saw the grapes, she said, "People have found black widow spiders in some of those bags of grapes; be careful."

Seeing for Yourself

Imagine or visualize what you'd like to create or experience and remind yourself that you have powerful abundant resources within you to support your vision. Bubble popping helps you clear your runway for takeoff or landing as you envision your next steps. Another way of seeing for yourself is when you see within yourself, what is also within another, even though on the outside, it looks different. This conscious practice increases clear seeing, which is a natural and authentic extension of ourselves that is foundational for living a life that is guided from our innermost wisdom.

Pragmatic Intuition

Pragmatic intuition is another everyday intuitive experience you can have or cultivate. For example, you hear the phone ring, or you hear a text come through, and before you pick up or look, you just know who it is. This is a frequent occurrence for myself and many others.

> ***You have dreams that give you helpful information, aligned next steps, or fresh insights.***

I once dreamed that my friend was getting tired of her job. I had no idea this was happening because she had never mentioned it and has always been devoted to her career. Then a week later I saw her, and she told me she'd been researching options to make a career shift. I dreamed my daughter and her friend were having fun hiking together. I told my daughter, and she said they were making plans to get together, but she hadn't yet told me about those plans. Right before my husband and I started dating (I already knew him), I dreamed about him and the next day there he was at a gas station in another town at the same time as me, and we made a plan to get together.

Once again, this kind of intuitive experience can just be a normal part of your life. It might be for deeper insights, and other times it might be just for fun.

Hearing on a Deeper Level

Your inner voice gently gives you supportive information or helpful messages on any area of your life. A negative, criticizing, self-doubting, or judgmental inner voice is not your intuition. Naysayer feedback contains old pictures collected along your life's journeys. They can be released or made into your own creative brand of comedy, to help you laugh it off.

With practice, you can normalize your inner guidance and use it to help you make clear and wise choices. Yet, intuition is not about knowing the outcome of everything ahead of time. This is why it takes courage to trust yourself on your spiritual path. Over time, this is where life experience comes in, where trust eventually distills into wisdom.

Receiving a *Hello* from Someone You Know Who Has Passed

The first time this happened to me was when I was in high school, and a classmate suddenly passed away. I knew the night before I was told that he had died. At the time, I felt like this was a goodbye yet now I know it was not just a goodbye, but also a *Hello*. This is a very common occurrence for people, whether they have consciously practiced being intuitive or not. Sometimes this kind of event can validate a person's awareness of being innately intuitive, and it also validates that we are more than just a body and can communicate on many levels.

When You Are Unconsciously Intuitive in a Helping or Healing Way

When you begin a conversation with someone that you think is just random chitchat, but you realize it's exactly what they needed to hear or know, even though you had no assumptions or preset ideas about what needed to be said, you just felt guided. You can also be on the receiving end where you feel amazed or healed by a conversation that someone initiates with you just at the time you most needed it.

As you recognize how healing or inspiring a seemingly random or unplanned conversation can be with someone, the world becomes an opportunity for deeper levels of appreciation and kindness that flow both ways.

Gut Feelings: An Intuitive Sign?

Your intuition isn't actually a "gut feeling." This is because it's in your mind and beyond your physical body. Gut feelings can be linked to your nervous system, which will automatically react based on past-time events, like a bee sting, dog bite, family trauma, or relationship breakup that happened long ago. This makes a gut feeling occasionally useful and sometimes misleading. Speaking in vibrational frequency or energy terms, if you rely too heavily on having a gut feeling, you'll stay in a more limited range of awareness. A gut feeling is vibrationally a step down from your pure intuitive knowing which makes it murky.

Imagine that you're at a party and you meet someone. Your body says loudly to you, *Wow, I'm really attracted to this person!* You have a strong gut feeling that you want to be with this person. Yet, if you say *Hello* to your intuitive knowing in this situation, you may receive a red light, not a green one. Your body may not easily distinguish the effect of another person's energy that is directed toward it, saying, *I want you.* Physical attraction, chemical reaction! Later on, you might say to yourself, *What was I thinking?* This is the source of many awkward hookups, some that even culminate in wedding bells.

If you give yourself a pause, ask, and then listen, your inner knowing can give you a direct, clear message, letting you know whether this encounter would be only a physical fling or have the potential for a deeper, long-term relationship. The more clarity you have about your decision-making, the more you ask the correct questions that lead to your becoming an ever *more* powerful conscious creator who is directing your own life! A similar type of scenario can happen when someone is trying to sell you a product you don't need or give you advice that may not be on your path. You might buy into it literally or figuratively, then afterward wonder, *What was I thinking?*

> *On a purely physical body level, it's well-known that a healthy gut biome can make you feel much better. Now that's what I call a healthy gut feeling! When you feel physically healthy, it's easier to feel enthusiastic about intuitive exploration and discovery.*

Ella's Story: Picking Up on Feelings

Ella was a deeply caring, intuitive coach with a background in education and conflict mediation. She took a couple of short training courses in a variety of healing modalities before beginning to advertise her services. Although Ella knew she would benefit from deeper intuitive training, she decided to delay her own inner work until she had more time to be a student. At first, things were going well because what she was sharing was beneficial. Yet, as the months progressed, she started to feel odd, like she wasn't herself. She felt some inner resistance toward her work, but it was hard to understand why. Ella felt mildly fatigued, yet all her bloodwork was totally fine; she was young and healthy. Ella also began to feel emotionally low, although she wasn't depressed (she'd checked in with her therapist on that). She just felt less enthusiastic, less powerful, less creative. Yet on the outside, she was still extremely functional. Intuitively she knew enough to know better. Also, she didn't like some of the relationships she was choosing that kept ending in drama or big misunderstandings. As an innately wise person, she wondered if changing her energy would help all this.

She decided to take some intuitive tools classes, to see what insights and healing might surface for her. Right away, she recognized that she was directing a lot more healing energy than she realized into trying to heal a few of her friends who were not yet interested in their own conscious inner growth. Ella also realized that in her work helping the public she was collecting everyone's energy on a bigger level than she had assumed, especially because of the way she was approaching her coaching work.

Ella just naturally used her feelings to *feel* what was happening with others as a way to support and guide them. In this way, you might say she was like a submarine pinging for those feelings through deep, murky waters. She had picked up this way of being when she was a young child through matching adults around her that she wished to heal and understand. On a vibrational frequency level, when she pinged an emotion from another "submarine" (person), sometimes she started to pick up on that sensation in her own space as more real than her own true feelings.

She had fallen into a pattern of telling herself that (as a professional) she knew enough to not do that which kept her from looking at what was actually happening within herself. Many emotions she pinged in others, matched up in subtle or unconscious ways with her own. Yet she wasn't consciously releasing any feelings. At that depth, it was hard for her submarine to distinguish between all she was receiving.

Through intuitive awareness classes, Ella learned to access her natural clear-seeing abilities. Now when she worked with people, she didn't over rely on pinging the feelings of others. Picking up on a variety of feelings is murky work because everyone carries the energy of emotions that don't belong to them. When you feel feelings as your primary mode of intuitive discovery, it's like sorting through a yard sale of stuff from many others. Aside from the physical and mental burden created from absorbing emotions from others, feeling feelings brings mixed insights. One insight is correct, but others are off. You are also more likely to resist feeling feelings when you unconsciously hit the ones that are yucky to you.

With training and practice, accessing her intuitive knowing and clear seeing is bringing Ella more neutrality and deeper insight with her coaching and work in conflict resolution. She has more space and gives more when she helps others, and she feels more enthusiasm in her daily life. She no longer feels fatigued or low and knows that she can stay in a vibrational frequency or space that brings clarity and healing for all parties, herself included.

Ryan's Story: Validating Unconscious Intuition

Ryan came to me because he felt anxious far more often than he'd like. His childhood was not the happiest, but as an adult, Ryan was a successful business owner, with his own lovely family. In our work together, I was able to highlight for Ryan that he was unconsciously intuitive and how that was impacting him. For years he'd been confused about what it meant to be intuitive. He carried bookmarked pictures that he had absorbed from scary movies or dramatized media portrayal.

Ryan applied his intuitive discernment to imagine a great idea that he translated through his creativity and intellectual skills into an ethical business. Sometimes while driving his car, he'd receive detailed original ideas out of nowhere which he then applied his business skills to make happen. Back in his office, he'd visualize an ideas board to try out creative iterations before creating a physical mock-up. He wasn't overly focused on monetary or material success; for him it was more about being an active creator for the highest benefit of all simply because that's what felt good in his heart and mind. He was engaging both his ability to clairvoyantly see and his intuitive knowing.

Ryan managed many employees, and, in his interactions with others, he always went the extra mile to be compassionate. He cared for people on a healing frequency of energy, improving the conditions of their well-being on a deeper level not easily quantifiable.

Because he was unaware that he was helping people from an intuitive-healing level, Ryan didn't realize that each time he helped someone, he absorbed some of their worries, stresses, fears, grief, and problems. *They* felt better, but on a baseline subtle energy level, he felt more anxious. Because he was a strong and focused person, he would override his anxiety and attribute it to his childhood. Because he didn't understand what it was to be intuitive and a healer, he thought he could outthink the whole situation. After all, he was a brilliant thinker.

In part, all of this related to Ryan's childhood because the bookmarked pictures remained from his experiences. When Ryan helped others with the same pictures congruent with his childhood, he absorbed some of those energies. For him, this energy absorption translated as anxiety, his go-to emotion from childhood. The feelings from long ago experiences were made real in the present. In this way, it was easy to trigger anxious feelings wired into his nervous system and confuse them with their origination.

Our culture unconsciously encourages us to possess our feelings as uniquely our own, as a way of self-identifying, so Ryan thought his anxiety had little to do with anyone else. His intellect alone could not rid him of his uncomfortable feelings. In fact, the more he wanted to get rid of those feelings through overthinking, the more they stuck, like glue.

I validated how his innate healing abilities helped many people and that he'd applied his intuitive knowing, envisioning, and creative abilities to establish a business that was beneficial to the world. Then I highlighted how, like an energy sponge, he was absorbing the emotions, thoughts, opinions, and bookmarked pictures of many of the people that he was helping. Hard as he tried, there was no way he could solve this at the level of intellect because it was an energetic, vibrational frequency.

I guided him to see how these actions showed up as a base level of personal anxiety energy that he could begin to intuitively, experientially recognize or highlight and release. We are all interconnected in an unseen type of ecosystem as energetic frequency through both our consciousness and unconsciousness (whether we like it or not). Effective solutions can't blossom from the energy space in which the problem was created.

It was an aha moment for Ryan to comprehend that he'd been carrying around everyone's weight of the world as vibrational frequencies to his own mental, spiritual, and emotional detriment. After this insight, he continued being the same compassionate and insightful man, but he had a new level of awareness. Validating and trusting his daily intuitive practices, Ryan was better able to distinguish and manage how energy from others could make him feel and think. He applied intuitive tools as a normal part of his busy day that supported not just him but everyone who interacted with him.

He began to care for himself on an energetic level, not just a physical one, and greatly reduced his anxious feelings. I can tell you some variation of this story countless times since it is what happens to intuitive people who don't appreciate how intuitive they are. Therapists, teachers, doctors, nurses, holistic health practitioners, parents, social workers, mentors, creatives, coaches, and leaders are examples of those who care deeply for the well-being of others and as intuitive people are susceptible to absorbing and carrying other people's vibrational frequencies.

Katie's Story: Recognizing Intuitive Cues for Decision-Making

Katie was simultaneously offered a professorial position at a prestigious university and a job at a small, relatively unknown state college. The prestigious professorial job paid more, and statistically would give her better opportunities for her career outlook. Katie's intellect presented an argument: *The data is obvious, take the job that pays more and gives you greater career opportunities.*

However, Katie's intuition told her to accept the job at the small state college. So, day after day, she sat with this key career decision, overthinking it, and feeling generally annoyed with her own laborious decision-making process. She swung back and forth like a heavily weighted pendulum, moving between survival thinking, data analyzing, and her quiet, intuitive knowing. Her intellectual training was wired to defend against and argue with her defenseless intuition by adding layers of complexity and effort. Still, Katie couldn't shake the inner guidance that was slowly moving her toward choosing the small state college while her logical brain screamed that she was being nudged toward career sabotage.

As a student, she had recently begun developing her ability to distinguish between her intellect and intuition, and how energy and pictures sent her into overthinking or overanalyzing. In a private session she laughingly began to see with more clarity what energies made her susceptible to indecision in specific areas of her life. One example was her pattern of using her unconscious intuition to read what others thought was best for her, rather than tuning to her own inner compass to guide her purpose. This had often caused her to be indecisive or a people pleaser. She agreed to stop second-guessing and give herself some inner space and trust. By pausing, she helped ground herself. She took a deep breath and expressed appreciation for the life she'd created so far, both the wonderful and the challenging events.

In this spaciousness, Katie knew the answer was to accept the position at the state college. Katie realized that fear was holding her back from listening to her inner knowing. More than that, it wasn't even *her* fear; it was the fear from the world at large that she'd mistaken as her own. Finding her own answers had been the real goal, yet she'd been trained to look everywhere *but* within.

Six months later, Katie met her future life partner, who also worked at the college. A year after that, she decided to become an organic regenerative farmer, applying her valuable scientific learning from her PhD to an agricultural ecosystem. Looking back, Katie realized her intellect could only analyze the data directly in front of her and wasn't capable of recognizing where her most valuable gifts could be put into action to fulfill her brightest purposes in the world. Katie's intuitive trust connected her with a literal and figurative ecosystem where she is happiest, personally and professionally.

Practical Model: Building Intuitive Trust

In the past when I was occasionally asked to be on selection committees at organizations, I experimented with my intuitive knowing to build more trust. To make the process more fun for myself and to practice simplified everyday intuition, I took the following steps:

1. I ground myself and set my energy in a high vibrational frequency such as enthusiasm, laughter, curiosity, appreciation, or joy, to open space and neutrality for inner guidance. Starting any process with overthinking or survival thinking does not allow for intuitive receptivity!
2. I meditate while grounded for about fifteen minutes to clear outside agendas, opinions, directives, assumptions, or collected emotions that might influence my intuitive observations of

what I see, know, or even feel. The goal is to be in a neutral space where I am aiming for the outcome that is in the highest good for that particular situation. More neutrality equals less unconscious preconceived judgments or assumptions. This helps me get past the surface levels that distract from deeper awareness and clear seeing.

3. I consider all the qualities valuable for this position. These qualities need to gel with the philosophy of the organization. For example, a love of their work, collaborative abilities for teamwork, compassion combined with an ability to handle a variety of road bumps, leadership skills in a specific area, and appropriate technical and intellectual skills. I now have my ideal list of qualities as if there were no budget constraints! This sets my sights on where I'm headed.

4. I make a list of the first and last names of the candidates, with no other information at all about them. During the first part of my intuitive discernment process, I sit with the list of names in front of me and apply a simple one to ten rating system for each candidate. I rate each candidate intuitively as I read their name to highlight the best match according to the qualities I'm seeking based on the organization's needs.

During this stage in the process, all I'm doing is reading energy. This is not a thinking thing (that is why it's not rocket science). A candidate who only scores a two might be a trustworthy person with tons of great life skills, but a low match for this particular role, or a low match with this group of colleagues in terms of personality traits or leadership/following styles.

This part of the process is completed without knowing anything about the candidate's qualifications, experience, or background. The whole point of this exercise and why I recommend it, is to see for yourself how intuitive you are. By practicing in this context, you can be instantly proven or disproven. You may feel like you are metaphorically solo sailing on the open ocean at thirty knots with no land in sight as you discover you have greater inner consensus of what you know and see.

5. Once I have my piece of paper with the names intuitively rated, I set it aside.
6. Next, I begin the more time-consuming, detailed, analytical process of carefully reading their résumés, references, and academic or work-related experience. This intellectual process confirms, or offers a differing view, of what I have initially discerned intuitively. For example, if a person received a high intuitive rating when I read the energy, the analytical process might confirm the reason for that. The ones with the highest ratings are the ones who came closest to meeting the qualities that I envisioned would make the best match for the job position. If I went into this without establishing what my mock-up is for a candidate, based on the needs of the organization, the outcome will not be very clear.

I validated my intuitive knowing each time I went through this type of selection process. When I eventually gathered with the rest of the selection committee to determine the best candidate to invite for an interview, my top choice was usually the committee's top choice.

I outlined this simple process to demonstrate a playful and safe intuitive decision-making tool that helps build a true friendship with your inner knowing. In this context, you are not solely responsible for the decision. Instead, you are part of a team, so it takes the pressure off. This kind of process can affirm your awareness in a practical way and remind you that you can read energy. You can apply a variation of this process without a team to find a better job, a new place to live, a preschool for your child, or an aligned relationship for you. When I train students to read energy, I sometimes have them read within themselves: "What energy is keeping me from knowing my own answers?" (in relation to a specific area they seek answers in). Or "What energy is causing me to feel this emotion that's bothering me?"

When you practice applying this intuitive strategy in your daily decisions, you may not immediately have 100 percent accuracy, but that simply means you need more practice.

With practice, you will build enthusiasm, clarity, and trust in your inner guidance. Validating when you have excellent intuitive discernment signals you to take it to the next level of awareness. Finding your space of neutral observation creates a healthy intuitive biome to read energy. Becoming more conscious of bookmarked pictures and releasing them, gets you there.

The Flip Side

Of course, sometimes consensus about the correct candidate does not happen within a committee. Once, the final candidates were presented to me by both name and their full résumés, which all looked exceptional. Yet based on my intuitive read, the top choice candidate was not going to be a good team player. This particular personality trait was not evident in the résumé or letters of recommendation. Nonetheless, I took the risk of looking foolish, or being told to butt out, and quietly gave my feedback to key members of the organization.

They weren't opposed to my feedback, but they were in a rush to make a decision. They felt they didn't have time to focus on interviewing more candidates. After all, as far as they were concerned, this candidate seemed like a good fit on paper and in person. Six months later, they asked this person to leave. The hire was a poor team player, and highly critical of others, which plummeted morale. All of this wasted a lot of valuable time and money in their organization.

When someone asks a question but is more invested in having you tell them what they want to hear, your intuition can guide you to validate the truth but communicate it with thoughtful diplomacy. Other times, you'll have clarity that it's unwise to engage in giving insight to someone who is not open to it because they are committed to a preset assumption or agenda. With practice, you can recognize whether and when they can handle hearing your insights.

> *Having strong discernment about people is applicable in all areas of life and takes practice.*

As you practice this skill, you leave behind old patterns that may blindside you. You learn to trust your intuitive decision-making skills through daily application. You are already becoming more intuitive by reading this book, because it opens your awareness to new experiences.

Recognizing Energetic Judgment Cues

Have you ever walked down a busy street and found yourself unintentionally staring at someone who really stands out to you, in some bright or positive way? You're not even sure why, but you know it's not related to feelings of romantic attraction or thoughts about their appearance. You simply have this unexplainable knowing about that person on an energy level. Your intellect can't quantify what is drawing your observational intuitive attention.

When a person draws your attention beyond physical presentation, investigate the quality of energy that is attracting your attention. Start trusting and validating your inner knowing in these moments as part of your ongoing intuitive discernment practice. Energy can also tune you into when you need to avoid something. As you practice giving your intuitive awareness space at the table, you'll tune in more easily to guidance which steers you away from situations, places, or people that are not beneficial.

Say someone walks toward you, and although you're innately a kind and thoughtful person, before you can stop yourself, you have an automatic set of inner reactions and judgments toward this person. You probably will blame yourself for having irrational, negative, or judgmental thoughts about this person.

What is happening? You know you're not actively trying to be judgmental, but a lot of bookmarked pictures show up! Rather than feeling ashamed, remember you can't be aware of every bookmarked picture (thought, emotion, opinion, assumption, or directive) that hangs out in your space and the judgment that results from it. As you begin to notice some of your judgments, consider it a quantum leap in awareness! Releasing this energy debris will greatly help you clearly discern with more neutrality what is happening. You will be able to determine: *Is this just a bunch of random mundane judgments collected from life's many journeys, or is there some useful information to recognize or act upon?*

The intellect-dominant culture likes to tell itself, "Oh I already know that." That and similar catch-all phrases keep us from looking deeper below the surface (*ahh big fish, scary!*). Recognize that you are experiencing awareness that you may not have words or context to describe yet.

Affirm your positive progress as you become open to new awareness. By now, you are conscious of how judgments result from patterns installed by familial and cultural conditioning based on intellect over intuitive awareness. Through consciousness you can rewire yourself and own your creative power to respond versus react. Ultimately, you're creating more space to have fun, be yourself, and let others be themselves too. You can even say to yourself, "That's just a bunch of bookmarked pictures and energies." Celebrate these healing moments. Intuitive awareness increases your choices and guides you toward finding your own answers!

Unsubscribe from the Judgment Game and Choose *Hello*

When my daughter was a toddler, I was walking with her down a quiet street when a woman walked toward us, swearing loudly, smoking a cigarette while arguing with someone on her cell phone. I braced myself to walk around her cigarette smoke and answer some toddler questions about what the F-word meant.

I had such strong judgments and inner annoyance because I was in protective mom-mode. In this moment, I forgot that whenever I put my energy into resisting something or someone I dislike, I unconsciously begin trying to solve the problem in my mind. The vibrational frequency of energy that holds the quality of resistance, dislike, or fear, sticks to me, to all of us, like glue. While solely focusing on this resistant problem (created from my judgment) I can't solve the problem until I change the way I focus my attention on it. It's a great opportunity to aim for a bit more neutrality and release some bookmarked pictures!

A person can behave and interact in an obnoxious manner, yet I have the choice to subscribe or unsubscribe to the bookmarked pictures and energy driving my judgment. I have the creative power to unsubscribe from the energy I invested in the problem. If you are trying to solve everyone's problems in your mind, or always be right, that's a sure symptom you are experiencing judgment, *not* intuitive awareness.

Intuitive awareness shifts you away from being stuck at the (vibrational) level of a problem, and gives you a springboard to imagine solutions, healing, and alternate possibilities. We can do this for ourselves, and we can do it for others. Especially once we stop seeing "others" as just a body that's different from our body, or an obstacle in our way on the street, or someone incapable of change because of outside appearances.

As the woman approached me and my daughter, I snapped back into the present moment knowing that I had a choice of inner response instead of emotional reactivity. I validated myself for consciously noticing my patterns. *Yay progress!* Then I could unsubscribe from the whole game, become a bit more neutral, and choose a different way forward.

I said a simple nonverbal *Hello* to what was brightest within this woman, whose behavior was just her book cover, not her essence as a human. I said *Hello* to the possibilities within her *and* myself, instead of emphasizing more of the same old patterns. This was a healing event for both of us, even if I was more aware of my choices and the impacts of my actions than she may have been. My response focused me in the present moment, transforming my thinking and feeling, while removing the whole idea of any problem that needed solving.

What Goes Around Comes Around

It is healing when you see another from your awareness of validation (*Hello*) in the
present moment rather than through old pictures. This powerful healing goes both ways. The person you are validating is empowered to choose some kind of transformation within their own mind as you

update to the present, allowing you additional space to know yourself and see your world. That's how simple healing can be when you are not in your intellect.

My story doesn't end here. Unexpectedly, validation arrived again. Several weeks later, walking down the same quiet street, the same woman walked toward us, smoking a cigarette, and talking on her phone. This time, she wasn't loudly cursing. And I felt calm and more neutral rather than resistant toward her energy. Progress!

As I prepared to move around her, simply to avoid the smoke cloud, before she got close to us, she extinguished her cigarette. Then she smiled at us for a brief moment and said a verbal hello to my daughter before passing by.

Only a few weeks earlier, I'd said a nonverbal *Hello* to her, and, on this day, we received a *Hello* back, simple as that. None of this could have happened if I'd stayed within the more structured framework of my intellect. By letting down a few walls, grounding myself, and staying in the present moment, I created an openness that led to both verbal and nonverbal communication, in active and receptive ways.

> ***Intuitive awareness increases opportunities for connection, goodwill, and other positive qualities.***

These kinds of experiences engage me with more awareness about the power of communication with the deep, subtle energies (the mycelia between people). Now when I walk in public places, I pay more attention to my random judgments, knowing that awareness can result in better outcomes all around me. All I need to remember is, "That's just a bookmarked picture."

Being aware is a practice of compassionate responsibility for your innate creative power. It can be applied in a million beneficial ways, even when society invalidates it.

Try it yourself. Validate how noticing a judgment is a signal that you are intuitively aware of yourself and your surroundings. Then, say *Hello* to what is brightest in you and those around you. It's an easy way to change the world for the better, one judgment and one person at a time.

Read the Energy of Your Body

Since everything is energy, you are intuitively reading energy whether you are conscious of it or not. You can read the energy of a career choice, person, or situation, read the energy patterns of judgment to heal and update yourself, or read the energy during a healing treatment for your body.

During a highly effective acupuncture treatment, I was lying on the table with tiny needles in my arms and legs, staring at the ceiling (since I could not hold a book or cell phone). I never studied acupuncture, so I had limited language about the practice of it. All I knew from past treatments was that I would ask for healing in a specific area, but the treatment would often be focused in an area that was not where I expected. *Hello* mycelia!

Feeling peaceful and without any distractions, I began reading the energy of my treatment. In the present moment, I became aware of the way the energy was moving through my anatomy. After checking in with my intuition about whether this feedback would be received with openness, I shared with the acupuncturist what I read.

In the reading, I included what physical anatomy areas the treatment was healing, the detailed directional flow of the treatment, as well as the quality of the energy as I had experienced it. He gave me a surprised look and said, "I could not have explained it better myself. That's exactly what I was treating."

It was a trust-building experience for both of us. I was validated for reading energy correctly, which led me to higher levels of trust in my intuitive abilities. He felt deeply seen as a practitioner. Leading with intuition positively affects not only your world, but the world around you. It gets you out of whatever bubbles you may have unintentionally formed around yourself so that you can communicate more dynamically.

Remember: Practice, Validate, and Repeat!

Practice removes effort. The energy of distrust, control, resistance, and self-doubt will bring your intuitive exploration to a temporary stop. Engaging experientially with intuitive awareness energy qualities such as enthusiasm, curiosity, creativity, generosity, willingness, laughter, honesty, and appreciation move you forward into spacious orchestration. Visualize filling yourself with a golden sun full of these qualities, anytime, anywhere, and let the simplicity of your inner knowing guide your practice. Every class I've ever taught on reading energy always begins with grounding yourself, being centered in your awareness, releasing some pictures, and setting your energy so that you can stabilize your space and become more neutral.

It's easier to have a dynamic relationship with your intuition in areas of your life where you have more confidence in your abilities. Everyone has these areas. These are the fields where you have developed trust over time, through repetitive experiences. Some of these repeat events have brought you favorable outcomes with less effort.

You don't always consider less effort areas to be significant because you're trained to focus on and fix what is not going well instead of celebrating what is going right. Your attention flows to what is hard and complex, or where you feel you are flailing or failing. The best way to build a balanced relationship with your intuition is by validating where it's effortless, and then applying it on an everyday basis in your harder (more effort) areas.

Pulling It All Together: How My Husband and I Practice

If my husband and I feel stuck knowing what's most aligned when we have an important personal, work, parenting, or family decision to make while on the go, we'll do an energy read of the situation, together. We've been doing this for nineteen years, so it's normal for us. Other situations might call for a much deeper or more extensive read, which we do as well (using advanced intuitive tools), but in this example, the goal is to keep it simple.

Depending on the situation, we might rate our choices on a scale of one to ten or assign each choice a red light (stop) yellow light (maybe), or green light (go), or simply assign a yes, no, energy quality or symbol (an emoji for example) to each choice. Other times we use the symbol of a single rose and read what happens to the rose when we ask the question: *Does the rose wilt or crinkle, or does it brighten and open under the sun in alignment?*

If we both receive the same answer, then it's pretty straightforward. If we each receive a different answer, we explore different possibilities. For example, one of us could be unintentionally reading the energy in past-time, and is being affected by emotional energies like fear, resistance, worry, or has an unconscious agenda, opinion, judgment, or assumption. This means one of us has unconsciously predecided the answer, or simply got distracted when we applied our awareness to see and know the answer. This process of discernment keeps us neutral, open, and curious, rather than seeking to be right or influence each other. It keeps us on track with our highest good.

Another variation that may occur is that we are both correct because we each received an answer that was orchestrated for us personally based on our unique experiences, goals, or needs. Or the answer we both receive relates to a different aspect of the same thing. In other words, one of us is reading the tail of the elephant, the other is reading the trunk. Other times, there are two equally beneficial possibilities, and it's a matter of choosing one of two great options.

No matter what happens, we can always ground, reset our energy, and simply read it again. Building trust in our intuitive decision-making, over a long period of time, means that we have a personal dataset confirming how effective this process is for us. It creates a foundation from which to grow, create, heal, and relate together. The process of reading energy together is not a serious job because that would drop our energy into dense effort, yet we might be reading something that is not at all a *light* subject or choice. Each time we make the space to read, we become more neutral observers.

My husband and I read energy together when we have an emotional conflict with each other. Let's say we are planning our busy week or cooking dinner. When one of us starts acting grumpy for no clear reason, the other person will say something like, "This doesn't seem like your energy." When this happens, we have a chance to read energy together, even if it's only two words and ten seconds of time. A likely response might be, "Oh yes, that was my friend's energy because I was just on the phone with him and he's having a rough day." This is a chance to reground, pop some bubbles, and reset to our own energy or frequency. We can apply intuitive tools to quickly shift energy into a more neutral space where we can be present and compassionate without absorbing or carrying around someone else's energy or unresolved problems. Then, we move on to whatever is next.

The practice of reading energy and pictures together has been the basis for a long-term relationship where we can have more neutrality, honest communication, and trust. Otherwise, we could easily end up unconsciously building up a wall of past-time unspoken and spoken judgments. This would divide us from really getting to the heart of who we are, and the ways we can grow both together as a couple and separately. Once again, none of this is about being perfect, because (in my experience) robust long-term relationships are always a lovely, messy work in progress. It's really about engaging your communication and awareness to improve upon the last creative iteration! This is also a way that we give each other energetic space.

Another example of what I mean in regard to giving each other space: Within weeks after my daughter was born, I remember thinking, *I can't believe she is going to grow up and actually move away someday.* Being a new mom, I felt more love for her than I could ever have possibly imagined. It makes sense that a few of the associated pictures in my mind translated to a sense of loss.

That's when I had an *aha* moment that reminded me: *The deeper you love, the more you must give space (as energy, not physical) to that person to thrive on their own path and grow into their own highest potential.* Often the more we love someone the more we are susceptible to unconsciously not giving them enough space to be who they are, on their path. A sure sign of that happening is when they push back or resist you as you try to help them. Giving a person you love more energy space is a relationship changer. It allows for a *closer* relationship that has space to keep growing. It lets in more laughter and light, too. I first explored that lesson involving love and letting go as a child the summer I spent with Sam.

It was spring and I was ten years old. I found an emaciated baby raccoon abandoned in the middle of the road near my house. I took her home and gave her a bowl of milk. Eventually she moved into my tree house; I named her Sam. She was free to go or stay but she did have room service. Every morning and evening I'd fry her some eggs. We'd go canoeing together, climb trees, she'd wrestle with the stuffed animals in my room, and take naps on my bed. Sam liked to climb up my legs and hug me. She also liked to climb up the side of the house next to the front door and reach her little arm toward the door handle. Her claw marks stayed for years beside the door.

By fall, she started to disappear for days at a time. I figured she was dating. I knew I had to let her be free, but I worried whether she had the skills to make it. I felt so much love for her, and a great desire to see her safely off into the wild, which was the best possible outcome for her. By late fall, she left for good. I spent the winter wondering if she'd found a mate and was able to survive in the wild. Then one spring night I was crossing a pasture with my father, and I heard a sound in the bushes. I could hear a whole group of raccoons, babies too. Sam came running over to me. She climbed up my legs and gave me an enormous hug! That was the last I ever saw of Sam. She was my first lesson in giving my heart to someone, then letting them go, so they could grow.

As a raccoon mom and later as a human mom, I realized that while naturally you hold your child close on a physical level, on an energetic level you have to give them more space each step of the way as they grow, so they have their autonomous space to see, be, and know while on their journey.

Intuitive Tools

Activity 1
Contrasting Bubbles: Read Energy in Present Time

This activity will give you the basics to practice reading energy, which will help with decision-making, emotional conflict resolution, healing yourself, or having deeper insight into your life or relationships. This first step will build trust in your abilities. The more you practice, the more validation you will receive! Then you can read the energy in any area of your life. Practice this exercise with a friend, partner, or by yourself as an effective and fun way to build trust in your intuitive awareness.

Directions

1. Sit in a chair with your feet on the floor. Give yourself three conscious breaths.
2. Say *Hello* to your amazing body by joyfully appreciating all the ways it supports you.
3. Greet yourself as the soul presence you are by appreciating your bright light and your power within. Say *Hello* to yourself! Quiet your analyzer by asking it to turn down the volume or intensity to an optimized, balanced level for you in the present moment.
4. Be centered behind your eyes in your neutral awareness in the present moment.
5. Ground yourself (Activity 1, Chapter 4). Set your energy in a high vibrational frequency, such as appreciation, joy, enthusiasm, humor, and/or playful curiosity, using the Golden Sun activity (Activity 1, Chapter 1).
6. Give inner permission for your awareness, imagination, and intuition.
7. Visualize a computer or movie screen four or five feet in front of you. This is your reading screen.

8. Imagine two bubbles, side by side, with some space between, on your reading screen.
9. Choose two feelings that you have recently experienced that contrast in some way, such as anger and joy, resentment and compassion.
10. Intend those two qualities show up as energy in the bubbles. Read what the energy is like (dense, light, heavy, bright, colors, other qualities).
11. Pop both bubbles and try it again with other qualities of energy. Enjoy whatever you discover and observe! You are reading energy, and this can expand into having experiences like I did at the acupuncturist, or like my husband and I have when we're on the go with decision-making or having a conflict as a result of energy in our space.

Activity 2
Intuitive Decision-Making

2 transition, a parenting-related decision, or considering a move to a new geographic location? As a practice to build intuitive trust, before you research these possibilities or visit a location in person, intuitively read your options as energy to discern your most orchestrated career move, professional help, place to live, etc.

Afterward, conduct intellectual (physical) research. Once you gain more physical details, or visit in person, you may find that your initial intuitive read matches quite well with your physical research. If it doesn't match up, no problem; keep practicing. This activity is an exercise in trusting and affirming your intuition and may be done solo or with a partner. With practice over time, this activity will train you to make aligned decisions on the go. Have fun!

Directions

1. Sit in a chair with your feet on the floor. Give yourself three conscious breaths.
2. Say *Hello* to your amazing body by joyfully appreciating how capable it is.

3. Greet yourself as the soul presence you are by validating your bright light and your power within. Say *Hello* to yourself! Quiet your analyzer by asking it to turn down the volume or intensity to an optimized, balanced level for you in the present moment.
4. Be centered behind your eyes in your neutral awareness, in the present moment.
5. Ground yourself (see Chapter 4, Activity 1 for more details). Set your energy in a high vibrational frequency, such as appreciation, joy, enthusiasm, humor, and/or playful curiosity, using the Golden Sun activity (Activity 1, Chapter 1).
6. Give inner permission for your awareness, imagination, intuition, and other similar traits.
7. Make a list of the characteristics you're seeking in a professional, or a list of ideal possibilities in career or geographical move options, or a list of qualities that support your child for their most beneficial outcome or positive healing (if it's a parenting-related choice). Perhaps you are looking for a professional with whom you can have easy communication or who is exceptionally knowledgeable and skilled in a specific area, someone you strongly trust who's capable of respecting you as a person, and who is understanding of your needs. Maybe you are researching people to date.

    To assist your research, you may ask questions like:
    a. What is the purpose of this relationship (or move or career change)?
    b. What are the ideal outcomes and qualities you imagine?
    c. How would you like to be supported or be able to thrive at optimal levels in relation to this professional, organization, new job, location, etc.?
8. You are establishing this ahead of time to consciously orchestrate your mock-up and your clarity about what you're seeking; it helps to set your energy and sights (envisioning) with your next steps.

9. Give yourself 100 percent permission to read the energy of this information in present time and apply your inner knowing for your highest-good decision.
10. Assign each option a number on a scale of one to ten, where one is low (not as close a match) and ten is high (a great match). Write these on a piece of paper next to the names/careers/geographic location options. You can alternatively assign each option with a red (no), yellow (maybe), or green (yes) color. Or assign a yes, no, or maybe to each option. You can also use the symbol of a rose and read what the rose response is, as energy. (For example, the rose stands bright and open under the sun, or it crinkles and droops.)
11. Conduct your intellectual research on these professionals, organizations, jobs, options, or locations.
12. Compare your intellectual research to your intuitive scores. See if anything stands out.
13. Meet your top two choices in person, on Zoom, or by phone (or perhaps you travel to a location where you'd like to move or visit a workplace to see what it's like). Compare again to your intuitive research. Any validation about your choices?
14. If any doubts arise about your intuitive ability, use the Popping Bubbles activity (Activity 1, Chapter 2).
15. Do this activity with a friend or partner (if they're open to it) for fun, so you can compare notes. Have your friend read the most aligned energy for you and then see if you have consensus.

Keep practicing! Fill yourself with a gigantic golden sun to validate your inner capability, knowledge, and awareness. (See Activity 1, Chapter 1 for more.) No matter the outcome, keep exploring this activity until it becomes second nature.

Chapter Six
Laugh Your Way to Easier Communication and Life Navigation

Humor and Laughter as Intuitive Tools

Sometimes I feel like I'm a laughter scientist observing the ways humor and laughter have dwindled to a limited resource in our abundant adult society. Laughter is the energy resource that comes naturally from children, yet it can quickly end up on the back burner as we mature.

Serious energy, including worry, self-doubt, resentment, self-comparison, inner resistance, and self-judgment, isolates people in their heads. Humor and laughter (expressed inwardly or outwardly) brings people together and opens doorways to the more expansive, intuitive mind. The serious intellect is no match for spaciousness, creative motion, and pure, joyous laughter.

Speaking of being a laughter scientist: In my early childhood, my father's job as a scientist was to increase the population of an endangered species of bird in New Zealand. He would occasionally take me to work with him, deep in the forest. An article was written about him, and it contains a photograph of him with my sister and me doing the serious work of helping to save an endangered species. I look like I'm having the most fun adventure of my life, smiling from ear to ear. Although this work was extremely challenging, my father would often pause and remember to laugh. I'm happy to share that the species is no longer endangered. The heavier or more serious the work, the more you will benefit from inner levity!

A heartfelt sense of humor is inclusive, expansive, silly, profound, and healing. These qualities have nothing to do with a person's ability to be entertaining, eloquent, or clever; rather, they are a way to reference a vibrational state of energy, experienced within you and by others

. Since laughter and humor are qualities of energy, they represent a type of creative power that opens space from overthinking. From this space, like a springboard, you can access the broader choices available from your intuitive awareness. In this way, the vibrational frequencies of humor and laughter are a tool for living life with more adaptability, range of communication, self-healing, and neutrality.

The Seriousness of Matching Energies

Have you ever noticed that sometimes you're having a great time by yourself, enjoying laughter or humor, until a certain, very serious person calls, texts, or visits, and you drop down to their state of energy, like a rock in a swimming pool? In that moment, you have matched that person's energy. Watch how easy it is to become serious around serious people. In my observation serious people sincerely don't intend to be so solemn, it's just an old pattern they dwell in, often fueled by feelings of responsibility. When they do shed that pattern, even for a few hours, their whole energy brightens like sunlight. The energy that brightens is their own because they have more space to be free (without becoming irresponsible at all).

> **Have you ever tried to manage a classroom full of laughing children? It's nearly impossible to be controlled by outside forces when you're engaged in laughter as a state of being. This is why the most loved teachers at a school usually have a sense of humor. The kids match them, they match the kids, and all goes more smoothly!**

Matching means you hold that same vibration as the person (place or situation), but that doesn't mean you start acting like them. Because you naturally are attuned to energy, you are impacted by it, whether you are aware of it or not. You can match the energy of seriousness, humor, drama, tension, joy, or any other emotion. Serious energy tends to be low vibrational and laughter energy is high vibrational, which gives you more creative or expressive range. For example, you might realize there's a serious situation that requires support, but if you just get stuck in the feeling about how serious it is, your enthusiasm drops so low that all of a sudden, it's hard to access any new ideas, solutions, or answers.

Remembering that you don't have to energetically drop into every drama or conflict you encounter can be very freeing. When you find yourself matching a serious energy, suddenly detoured from a lovely day, it can distract you or throw you off from being present. Because you don't like the feeling you are having, you might push against the other person or situation in an effort to set an energy boundary. This is resistance energy.

Or you may feel overwhelmed because you have identified with that low vibrational frequency and are temporarily disengaged from your own true feelings. Or you might override this matched energy, pretending it doesn't exist as you tell yourself that you are "just fine" (although your intuitive knowing is telling you otherwise!). All these reactions are signs that you have matched serious energy with somebody else.

You can also engage serious energy entirely within yourself. If I take myself too seriously when I'm starting a new project, energetically my collaborative systems begin to malfunction. Children rebel against this kind of energy, but so often, adults match it, and then everyone is dead serious, slowing down all dynamic movement and healing to a snail's pace. Serious energy is essentially a boring energy; it's not spacious or dynamic, and it lacks movement or range. When children don't receive a fun or interesting assignment to put their energy into their highest creativity, they may instigate chaos as a form of resistance against serious energy.

Resistance energy can also look like those times when you spend a lot of unnecessary effort bumping against the restrictions you've imposed on yourself. While living in a tight box of few choices, you lose sight of where you're headed, and what could become possible if you maintained a wider lens through your brightest awareness. Serious energy can make it hard to hear yourself or anyone else and is often accompanied by a predecided opinion or assumption (I'm right or "I already know all this"), which serves to protect, or the comparison type of protective thoughts ("My bad situation is worse than your bad situation"). Sometimes so-called problems even relate to having many choices, but not accessing your inner knowing to choose what is aligned or most healing.

> ***Simply noticing what it is like to match serious energy as it occurs within you represents extraordinary awareness. It's as simple as that! Witness it, along with the underlying bookmarked pictures running your show and watch your energy shift in the moment.***

When you notice that you're matching energies with an unwanted drama or stress, for example, you can ground and stabilize your emotional, spiritual, physical, and mental levels of awareness. After giving yourself a pause from your serious energy, unsubscribe from the drama or stress by shifting your energy to a higher vibration, such as inner laughter, joy, curiosity, abundance, compassion, or self-love. This new, conscious choice comes from the spaciousness of your inner knowing, "knowing" how to navigate the rough terrain of life!

Match Laughter to Transform Seriousness

Is this easier said than done? Nope, it really isn't rocket science. How do you shift matching energies that are not serving you? Humor and laughter. Remember the last time someone started laughing, really hard? Did you start laughing too? Recall how easy it was to match laughter with laughter; you probably couldn't have stopped yourself if you tried! Or what if you're at a movie or dinner party and you start laughing but then everyone else has stopped laughing so you are now trying to contain your laughter? *That* is easier said than done.

> **When you laugh, whether deep within yourself or boisterously with friends, children, family, or work colleagues, you alter your vibrational frequency in a profound way.**

Expressed either nonverbally or verbally, laughter creates space for you to slow your overthinking chatter and survival behaviors. From this pause, you can respond from your bright awareness instead of reacting from your old patterns.

Often the busier you get, the more serious you get, like you are on a life-or-death hamster wheel! The more solemn you are, the more you feel responsible for everyone and everything, even while you know intellectually it's not possible to be accountable for everyone and everything! As you get busy and serious, all your extra resources seem to fall away because your efforts are in trying to survive each day (*Hello* survival thinking).

Yet it's possible to be in a humorous state of being while navigating the challenging landscapes of your everyday existence. Self-critical thinking, drama, and stressful feelings are no match for inner laughter. As a healing frequency of energy, laughter transforms stuckness, bringing movement to rise above overthinking, survival thinking, fear, or feeling victimized by the choices available to you in a given situation.

When I gave birth to my daughter, nothing went as planned. A very long labor led to an unexpected C-section. By the time I was getting prepped for surgery, I was more exhausted than I'd ever been in my life, and all my hopes of an ideal birth were seemingly dashed. My pregnancy was completely unremarkable medically speaking yet I had intuitively known that the birth wasn't going to go well. No matter how I had thoughtfully prepared for the big day, hoping my intuition was somehow incorrect, still it went the way it went. There was no evidence of this prior to the birth so the best I could do was be (literally) right next to the OR in a hospital birthing center (best of both worlds, at least in my case). As they prepped me for surgery, I was feeling only deep love and gratitude. I could not help but find incredible humor in that present moment as I released thousands of old, bookmarked pictures that I had absorbed on my life journeys relating to the "ideal birth" and "how to raise your child." My daughter seemed to be saying, "Mom, let's clear out and update your whole spiritual ecosystem for my arrival, because it'll makeq raising me much easier if you don't get stuck in those old patterns." It was an extraordinary healing because it was about so much more than just the circumstances of a physical birth. Like mycelia, everything is interrelated. In this state of exhausted surrender and divine love mixed with laughter, I started to crack a few jokes with the surprised doctor and nurses. I felt completely supported by everyone there. Soon, my daughter was in my arms, healthy, peaceful, whole. That's about as ideal as you could ask for! Every birth is equally miraculous in its own unique way, no matter how it goes.

This was a complete reboot in my spiritual approach, changing the way I orchestrated my life as a soul-body team. My inner laughter and humor were essential tools to help me navigate this shift. I had moved through so much of my life engaged in creation without consciously giving myself a receptive space to harmonize the active and receptive energies. I had been matching the dominant intellect culture of doing, doing, doing and overlooking the inner teamwork that blossoms when you access the full power of both active and receptive energy in relationship to yourself. I was also frequently undervaluing my capability, gifts, and skills. This experience taught me that when I give space for divine orchestration, everything moves with love in a spaciousness that is truly hard to put into words, and it doesn't always happen the way I plan it. Being intuitive is a receptive state of being and I was experiencing a new level of receptivity and creative orchestration in all areas of my life.

Releasing all those pictures made space for having a ton of fun and ease as a new mom, giving freedom for my daughter to move with her own brand of creative orchestration to be the powerhouse that she is. It also helped me to have much deeper compassion and insight when I worked with parents and soon-to-be parents. Regardless of what kind of birth you have, there is nothing quite like becoming a new parent to light up all your "perfect" (like "failure" for example) and "responsibility" pictures, and every other kind of connected, long-held picture, imaginable. Your children light up all your old pictures for at least the first eighteen years, so your sense of humor and your willingness to celebrate the way healing shows up in your life on a daily basis is paramount.

Laughter is always available as a quality within you, waiting to be expressed. You experience the depth of laughter's high vibrational frequency within and beyond your body. When you sprinkle the key ingredients of humor and levity into your journey, you can experience inner comedy that builds resilience.

The Value of Humor and Laughter

Most of us seek and welcome laughter and humor. Yet rarely do we respect the genuine value humor and laughter give to every aspect of our lives. Nothing sticks to you while laughing. Perhaps that is why we don't give this state of mind enough credit, because there's nothing to hold onto. Anything that can't be counted or quantified falls low on the hierarchy of importance in our culture. Along with other immeasurable qualities, such as kindness, imagination, intuition, compassion, and generosity of spirit, humor and levity don't cost anything, even with inflation.

As you collect your "laughter data," observe people who nurture these highly valuable qualities in their lives. Sometimes a speaker, moderator, leader, or teacher instantly elevates the energy of a group with a few small comments. A humorous quip changes the energy with your friend, spouse, or child when things get too serious and stuck. Then, you are in a relationship of humor and laughter, which raises the vibrational frequency of the entire situation. The focus moves away from being stuck at the same level of the problem, and serious energy dissolves into more expansive territory. A pause can then provide space to see, know, imagine, create, communicate, or experiment with openness.

Matching Inner Laughter

Inner laughter is one of the most useful tools you can have. Let's say you're listening to a podcast while driving, and although the content isn't deep, it's precisely what you need to hear.

You might be smiling while listening, but on the inside, your inner laughter is fully ignited. Your energy changes as you shift from serious vibrational energies and match this laughter energy.

Then you head into a stressful workday, uncomfortable appointment, or awkward family gathering. Some of that vibrational frequency remains with you for hours ahead, changing your inner landscape and increasing your resiliency to meet these challenges with a higher energy level.

In this way, as your inner levity creates more outer laughter, you also subtly affect others' energies. When you recognize and validate your inner laughter, you'll give unspoken permission for others to match you, rather than *you* matching *their* seriousness. Likewise, if you acknowledge that you are unintentionally bogged down in solemn energy, you can consciously match someone who holds an inner laughter frequency, which instantly elevates your energy frequency. You simultaneously attune to that authentic energy that's innate within yourself.

Engaging your inner laughter allows you to see broader perspectives. For example, in emotionally painful moments, when people have a laugh together, they begin to heal. Everyone involved has a renewed opportunity to communicate more deeply and honestly from who they truly are, not just who they are being in the world to survive.

Inner laughter creates space for you to just be and gives permission for others to do the same. You become more compassionate in your responses, listen with greater enthusiasm (to hear more), and invite others to collaborate with you. Things go more smoothly, as part of a spacious orchestration that plays a symphony for you.

Consciously Match with Laughter

Unconsciously matching low vibrational frequency equals getting stuck or entangled in drama, emotions, choices, or behaviors that are not orchestrated for your most joyful life. People unconsciously match media, news, advertising, organizations, and politics all the time, which pinballs them around in random directions. Think of the billions of snippets of every kind of information launched at you on social media. It's easy to fall out of your grounded vessel, following those fast-paced messages down into dark depths, or up into the clouds, if you remain unconscious of where they are taking you. Many self-destructive behaviors begin with an unconscious match.

Becoming conscious of the ways you are *un*conscious is always a work in progress, rather than a neat and orderly queue. You might begin by laughing at the comedy of it all. Now that you have shifted into a higher vibrational energy, perhaps more of you will agree, *It is definitely possible.*

Let's say you are helping a dear friend who is experiencing some serious emotions that you have heard many times before. You don't wish to invalidate your friend's feelings by suggesting they change to a different topic, but you'd also love to see them feel better. At the same time, you'd like to stay in your own high vibration instead of matching your friend's serious energy. *Hello!* You have an opportunity to consciously choose to keep engaging your inner levity in the face of your friend's somber energies, even without smiling.

As you chat with them, observe your own state of inner laughter. Experience this quality within yourself. This is your state of being, and your energy is not resisting, rejecting, fixing, judging, controlling, or dropping into your friend's state of being. Your energy becomes neutral, as if you are simply noticing the chair you are seated in.

Because everyone (unconsciously or consciously) feels or relates with energy, on an intuitive level there is a good chance that your friend will tune into your inner laughter energy. This will elevate their energy in subtle ways, such as becoming more introspective, less charged up and ungrounded, or even laughing a bit about what's going on. This starts to transmute your friend's experience into something new. Your friend will match your energy, if you decide that you don't have to drop into their inner state of energy. This is a compassionate state of being.

Inner Work: Lighten Up to Go Deeper

Often when we hit a serious energy match, we immediately become stern or defensive. Humor and levity can instantly diffuse or neutralize this rigid energy state and create a healthy, intuitive biome for your inner work.

Some people approach their inner or spiritual growth with the same energy they approach their professional training: by setting high goals for themselves. This makes sense in the context of a test-based system founded on competition and accomplishment: Work hard, rise to the top, and your ego is rewarded. The message becomes: In order to take yourself seriously, and for others to take you seriously, you must do serious work.

You are often expected or trained to equate "deep" with serious, yet in order to do the "serious" work of inner growth, it makes an enormous difference when we lighten up, vibrationally. The high vibrational energies of your intuitive awareness, creativity, and imagination are the seat of your power, and they may take cover in the face of all this seriousness.

> *Lightening up to go deep relieves you of the intellectual structures and bookmarked images that close down your awareness. Inner work accesses your power to heal.*

> **Humor and laughter support you in this journey.**

When I navigate any communication that is a bit sensitive or requires solution-oriented creativity, if I don't tune to the frequency of humor or laughter, I will have to work three times harder to make beneficial progress. Whether I'm directly speaking with someone or putting it in writing, energy is energy and translates through the airways, all the time. I'm sure you've attended a work meeting or answered the phone and received a blast of energy from someone who lost their sense of humor. Or you've read an email or social media post that came through like a Harry Potter howler message. *Ouch!* You can even end up with a headache, sore neck, or sore back from that energy.

Imagination to the rescue! Envision an inner humor or laughter meter and turn the dial on high *before* you respond.

Aim for Neutrality

How does consciously matching or engaging with humor and laughter *create* neutrality? In this intuitive context, neutrality is a space of nonresistance to a situation or person you can't control. Neutrality creates space for some kind of new experience, a transformation. When you are in a neutral space, you are aware of your environment, relationships, and emotional state, yet not polarized into right or wrong, good or bad, assumptions, resistance energy, or preset agendas. Maybe a situation sucks, but since hating it digs you deeper, you choose a neutral state of being. If you are in a more neutral space, when something irritates you or makes you feel rejected, you will find that you don't attach a lot of extra judgment, drama, or resistance to it, since that closes off your ability to respond and act in an effective way. Resistance energy has a way of making a single feeling (i.e., I'm so annoyed at my colleague/friend/partner) more real or primary than your other amazing inner resources.

Humor and laughter engage your energy in a more neutral space. From this open space, there is room for greater choices to communicate (or not) and clearer observation, and from this openness within springs a place of acceptance. Acceptance doesn't mean giving up. In this context, acceptance creates even more space for change. It's like saying, "Okay, here we are. What's next?"

Perhaps you spill coffee on your new suit right before an interview or your son called from the principal's office… on your one day off that month. Or maybe your basement floods, or you receive a medical bill you can't afford, or you detonate an emotional explosion in your family because you know you need a divorce. Comedy is not separate from life, even though it's easy to label these scenarios as completely humorless.

This is precisely where the practice of inner laughter and activating your sense of humor is essential. You begin by consciously choosing humor and levity, first to upgrade your energy frequency, and eventually, to find a space of neutrality. And by the way, don't judge yourself when you have a humorless day. Instead, just say *Hello* to your bright light, and remember your inner power.

Grow your neutrality as you move into the flow of compassion for yourself and others. Witness this spacious orchestration unfold where you are supported or assisted in ways you can't always anticipate ahead of time. Trust yourself. Consider how giving inner permission for this space to open moves you into an orchestration that supports you.

In Chapter five, while in protective mom-mode, I dropped into serious energy and resisted the energy of the woman who was smoking a cigarette and swearing on her phone. I saw my judgments and I chose to validate myself for noticing them, instead of telling myself that I was above judgment. I now know that when I judge others, it is a fantastic opportunity to heal a matching judgment of myself. In this case, that energy match involved my desire to control the space around myself to protect my daughter. In that moment I also read the energy of the woman, and her match was *her* desire to also control the space around her, to make herself feel safe in the world at large (not directly in relation to me). In many obvious ways, we were "different," and I could have easily claimed that we had nothing in common.

By the next time I saw her, I had become more neutral within myself to that energy match. By disengaging my serious resistance to this woman's energy, I created space for both of us to communicate and feel safe. In the case of this woman, my neutral energy (popping some bubbles containing my judgments) opened the door for an improved energetic interaction for all of us. There is no telling what might happen when you spot and change your energetic matches. *Hello*! I'm using this example because it was such a minor, everyday interaction. I know that anyone can find a similar situation in which to practice within themselves, beginning with a little inner levity; no talking required. I know many people who consciously bring this quality into their work as mental health therapists, healthcare practitioners, parents, teachers, business entrepreneurs, creatives, and leaders.

Muppets: The Healing Energy of Neutrality

When my daughter was five, she woke me up at 4:00 a.m. because she was about to throw up. I sat next to her beside the toilet while she waited for the big event. We all know that wretched pre-puke feeling, and there's nothing fun about it. I don't recall ever having an inner sense of humor during this special toilet-side time when I was her age.

Right before she threw up, she asked me, "Who's that funny drummer from The Muppets?" Apparently, the YouTube Muppets video we had watched earlier clearly had had an effect on her. "Animal," I said. "He's so funny," she laughed.

Right away, I saw my daughter was not making a big deal out of her situation. She wasn't resisting her uncontrollable body movements by pushing back (*Oh no, this is so awful!*) or pitying herself (*Why me?*). For her, it was no big deal, and I saw that this was her experience of neutrality and acceptance.

I'd seen something similar watching kids at a soccer game when one child temporarily injured her leg, but because she was so excited about playing, she related to the injury in a no-big-deal way, immediately letting it go in her mind, and soon her body followed. Yet from my perspective, I was thinking, *Ouch, that must have hurt!* I had seen adults hurt themselves in more minor ways and react angrily like they'd just been beaten up by the couch they bumped their toe into, or the toy they tripped over. I thought to myself, *This is what we do in our overthinking minds, quietly, about all kinds of events, experiences, people, and places we encounter.* We add extra to it; we make it a big-fish story. Sometimes the fish gets bigger each time we tell it. Our creative power builds it, and keeps building it, until we make a new conscious decision.

Back to the toilet: Once my daughter threw up, it was back to bed. She felt pretty good in the morning, and never even mentioned puking. She was completely released from her experience the night before. She had attached absolutely nothing extra to this situation. I didn't bring it up either, because why rehash it and make it a big-fish story?

Observing her, it was clear that when we don't attach extra negative or serious thinking to events out of our control, it's easier to get through them, even when you know it kind of sucks! Even better, it's easier to release the energy of that event when it's over. My daughter demonstrated how the energetic frequency of neutrality and laughter helps transform suffering.

The Neutralizing Effects of Inner Laughter

One time when my daughter was five, I noticed she was getting rapidly sick with a bad cold. We had important plans the next day, so my mind immediately filled with worry about what was in the future. Still hoping for the best, I gently asked if she felt like she was getting a little bit better. She paused for a moment, and then wisely said, "I might get better, I might get worse." Despite the uncertainty of her statement, my mind perked up, suddenly intrigued by the energy of her words, which sounded calm, peaceful, and neutral. Although she was not laughing or referencing funny things, her energy still had the quality of inner levity. My daughter was in a state of neutrality with complete acceptance of the situation.

As an awareness teacher, I'm a person who observes energy, patterns, healing, communications, and creativity for a living, so it's fun to learn something new every day! I matched my daughter's neutral space and the energy of her inner laughter. I saw how I'd rapidly fallen into the rut of worrying, which was not healing for either one of us and was actually a kind of big-fish story, making something from nothing. Even when I spoke soothing words, my words still matched my serious energy, and this is the energy that my daughter, luckily for me, did *not* match. *Hello grounding!*

Best Case Scenario: Conscious Use of Intuitive Tools

One summer, my young daughter broke her arm at day camp. I arrived at the emergency room soon after she did, and my sister was already there. The EMT from the ambulance told me how amazingly calm and communicative my daughter was on the ambulance ride, especially as they had not given qher any pain medication. He described how she was joking with him, even though her break was bad enough to need the bone reset (twice, over six hours, as it turned out). She recited the words to "Weird Al" Yankovic's parody song, "Like A Surgeon" to him. He couldn't believe she had the grounded presence to be in a space of inner laughter during an ambulance ride, at age nine!

The emergency room was chaotic and included several police who had to restrain a person who had lost all control. Immediately upon arrival I grounded myself so that I could be present, calm, and clearheaded, despite the chaos. I practiced my neutrality by bringing in some golden suns with the energy of compassion. As a mom, my reactionary instinct is to fall into sympathy overload (I feel your pain). By now I had learned how this reaction is unhelpful for my daughter (or anyone), since it's a serious energy load on her that doesn't allow space for levity.

The funny thing was that my daughter had already effortlessly set the stage for levity and neutrality before I had arrived because the energy of her communication in the ambulance had stayed with her when she entered the emergency room. She was interacting with doctors and nurses who were complimenting her, astounded that she was able to remain centered and grounded, despite the disconcerting floppy, broken arm about to be reset. Out of the blue, one doctor came in and started cracking corny jokes; maybe he missed his call as a stand-up comedian. As it turned out, the staff was happy to match my daughter's inner laughter!

After a grueling six hours, and two bone resets, we headed home. The entire episode affirmed the power of intuitive tools like inner laughter, neutrality, grounding, and golden suns. It was incredible to witness the way my daughter led all of us with her powerful energy presence. Whenever we communicate from our authentic presence, that *Hello* is a healing for all. It's like saying, "I see your whole being. I see your light." I have traveled the world, and I love being surprised at who naturally communicates on that level. Often, it's people who are grounded and at home in their bodies, which allows them to be present.

Recently my daughter was reviewed on her contribution during a week-long event away with a large group of teenage peers. Her teachers said, "She was a force of positive energy for the group throughout the entire week. One of the most awesome and impressive things about her is her willingness to sit down and have a conversation with anyone, and to approach those conversations with genuine openness and curiosity. Her engagement and leadership set a positive example for everyone." There are a lot of other young people like this in her friend groups, in our communities, and throughout the world. They have the power and knowledge to be a bridge between ancient wisdom and the modern, technology-oriented society and culture to help restore balance, each in their own areas of purpose.

Laughter Therapy for Serious Parenting

Eve felt that when Chris took his turn being the primary caregiver, he was forgetful about little details and not as careful as she was. Chris felt like Eve's expectations were unreasonable, and that she didn't give their son enough physical space to explore. The love they shared for their son (and each other) was clear, but the *way* his care should be implemented was where they had different pictures.

Because they hadn't yet consciously discovered and established what energy they wished to create from as parents in present time and as a team, they were more susceptible to all the advice overload that was hanging out in their space. There were plenty of times when they appreciated good advice, but this was too much information. This load of opinions as energy was in the communication space between them, without their awareness, causing them to judge each other, rather than be a unified team.

Before becoming parents, they had clear and direct communication with each other. Now their parenting conversation was being detoured through a bunch of debris that showed up as resentment directed toward each other. The bookmarked, fear pictures that engaged their unconscious awareness felt totally real and that each of them was right. They were polarized into two different parenting camps, yet neither Chris nor Eve was fully comfortable in their camp. They both felt a strong need to do this right because their parents had both divorced when they were young kids.

When Eve watched Chris forget stuff or when she saw him not watching their son closely enough as he explored the house, she got very serious. Likewise, when Chris watched Eve following their son around and not letting him explore enough, he got very austere with Eve, feeling that she was overbearing. They needed to reset the energy of their own current family space, incorporating their parenting styles into the present. They were paying attention to long-held pictures that were polarizing them from giving each other space to find appreciation in each parenting style a little differently.

Eve and Chris learned some intuitive tools that opened their awareness and created more space for them as a family. They laughed as they recognized how many of the old pictures about being right were really just what-if, fear scenarios. They especially enjoyed a guided visualization exercise where they imagined the energies of seriousness and laughter or humor. *Vive la différence!* They realized that whenever they said *Hello* to their son on a healing level rather than just a body level, he started to laugh.

After that, whenever they watched each other with their son, they'd consciously fill themselves with laughter energy, bringing some levity into the situation instead of getting stuck in a serious rut. This levity raised their vibrational frequencies, individually, as a couple, and as a family. Laughter allowed them to meet each other halfway and come to a deeper place of valuing their differences and commonalities as parents. Chris stopped forgetting to feed their son the vegetables, and Eve started to give their son age-appropriate levels of space to explore. And they both understood that they could match the delightful laughter energy of their son *and* let him be the laughter leader in the family! This equaled positive growth for everyone.

How Changing Your Energy Changes Others' Behaviors

Jen was close to her brother, but her sister-in-law displayed irrational anger outbursts regularly at most people around her, including insulting Jen on a frequent basis. This was a serious situation because it certainly wasn't funny! Jen would get deeply solemn on the phone, trying a combination of reasoning with her sister-in-law, drawing healthy boundaries, and trying to change the subject to better conversation topics. Nothing worked.

Jen's sister, Meg, was also close to their brother. Meg no longer had the same serious situation with this sister-in-law. Now, before interacting with her sister-in-law, Meg grounded herself, said *Hello* to her own bright soul presence, and connected with her inner laughter. She bumped up her vibrational frequency of inner laughter by visualizing a humor meter. She imagined a funny scene or watched a few minutes of comedy on Netflix to change her inner energy approach to her sister-in-law. Their conversations on the phone were usually brief and reasonably courteous; that was all. No insults. Granted, they weren't close with one another, but the goal was to have a civil relationship. Once she'd set her energy in this way enough times to embody it, she could instantly tap into that energy as needed.

"What is your secret?" Jen asked Meg one day. Meg told Jen that she realized she couldn't change their sister-in-law, but she was in control of transforming her own resistant reactions into responses through humor and levity. She approached the preparation for each conversation playfully, not seriously, to establish high frequency energy that their sister-in-law might match at some level. It was working!

Jen tried this change of energy within herself. For five minutes, she imagined bucket loads of laughter energy showering into her space while doing dishes. She visualized setting her overthinking chatter on a shelf like a nice hat, so she could stop feeling defensive, resistant, and trying to fix what she couldn't fix. After this process, Jen discerned feeling less apprehensive, but she couldn't exactly distinguish the energy match. However, simply filling herself up with laughter actually felt amazingly refreshing, even rebellious in a silly way.

> ***What? I can just do this? This is easy! I thought it had to be complex!***

Spontaneously, she called her brother's house, and her sister-in-law answered. "Hello," said Jen, "How are you?" She was still imagining showering herself with 100 percent laughter energy, and she felt a sense of ownership of her personal space and body, without a need to defend it.

"I'm okay," said her sister-in-law, in a disinterested way. "I'll let your brother know that you called. I gotta go."

That was the beginning of a very uneventful relationship between Jen and her sister-in-law. The relationship was not conversationally fulfilling, per se, but was now emotionally diffused, with no more drama. The anger energy had nowhere to stick anymore, at least when aimed at Jen, who was now in a place of possibility, matching her own inner laughter and humor energies.

An unexpected gift arrived as a result of Jen igniting her inner levity. This new creative process transformed her energy in relation to her employees at her workplace. She began to apply her inner laughter energy in ways that created a lot of mobility or range in relation to communicating directly and honestly as a boss, without offending those around her. She observed repeatedly that people could actually quite literally hear or listen more closely when she spoke from this vibrational frequency. They were also more likely to respond by taking inspired action. Engaging her own inner laughter brought a new level of collaborative teamwork to her company.

Pause: Stop Taking Yourself So Seriously

When you practice humor and laughter as an intuitive tool, you give yourself opportunities to navigate with more ease and finesse in the world. By now you know it's not an exclusive club with high fees! This innate tool, and your skill using it, can be developed and honed. It's never too late to shift your vibrational frequency to this way of being.

Engaging this frequency within yourself lets you authentically express it (verbally or nonverbally). Yet to get there, it doesn't matter if you begin through simply saying *Hello* to this frequency within yourself, or by watching a funny movie, singing, through fun hobbies, running a few miles to get your energy moving (exercise can lead to laughter), being in nature, or through faking laughter (which leads to real laughter). Eventually you will experience it from within yourself as a vibrational frequency of healing energy.

If your job is so serious that smiling would look strange, incorporate an inner smile. Imagine smiling within yourself for no particular reason. When we unconsciously participate in the intellect culture, it's easy for us to unconsciously match serious energy. When we consciously participate, we can choose. That way, if you actually prefer serious energy, at least you know that's really your genuine preference.

Appreciate that as you apply your intuitive knowledge in the world, you cultivate constant growth which can equal continual upgrades to your baseline of joy or happiness. Transforming a repetitive or tricky bookmarked pattern that's not working for you involves willingness to pause and stop taking yourself too seriously for a moment. That way, you can raise your vibrational frequency to a fresh level of illuminating creativity. This can be as simple as giving yourself permission to have fun envisioning and imagining! Affirm that you have incredible awareness within yourself and the power to transform through your intuition and creativity.

Intuitive Tools

Activity 1
Laughter Meter

A laughter meter is an excellent way to track your levels of inner laughter when you encounter a very serious person, place, or situation, or when you feel stuck in serious energy, rehashing old conversations or overanalyzing. The laughter meter helps you pinpoint the causes of both serious and laughter energies, allowing you to consciously choose to unmatch from those energies that hold no value for you, and match worthwhile energies, to better serve you and others.

Make sure your meter always stays high enough to meet the demands of your day. The more stressful, challenging, or busy day you are having, or the more you feel irritated, angry, guilty, overwhelmed, excluded, sad, or fearful, the higher your laughter meter should go. Remember: The easiest way to increase your laughter meter… is to laugh! In this activity you will imagine a laughter meter or make one out of cardboard as a physical symbol, while discerning various serious and laughter energies in your life.

Directions

1. Sit in a chair with your feet on the floor. Give yourself three conscious breaths.
2. Thank your amazing body by joyfully appreciating all the ways it is a vessel for your laughter to be expressed.
3. Greet yourself as the soul presence you are by validating your bright light and your power within. Say *Hello* to yourself! Quiet your analyzer by asking it to turn down the volume or intensity level to an optimized, balanced level for you in the present moment.
4. Be centered behind your eyes in your neutral awareness, in the present moment.

5. Ground yourself (Chapter 4, Activity 1). Set your energy in a high vibrational frequency, such as appreciation, joy, enthusiasm, humor, and/or playful curiosity, using the Golden Sun activity (Chapter 1, Activity 1).
6. Imagine a laughter meter that ranges from 0 to 100 percent. Or physically mark your cardboard meter with a range from 0 to 100 percent.
7. Recall a situation or person that always makes you laugh or at least smile.
8. Ask the laughter meter: How much inner laughter energy do I have in this area?
9. Watch the meter show you the percent of laughter you have in that moment. Validate the truth of this experience for yourself! Then, imagine placing your meter with that percentage inside an imaginary bubble, and pop it so it dissolves.
10. Choose a person or situation that makes you lose your inner levity and drop down to serious energy.
11. Envision a new laughter meter. Ask: How much inner laughter do I have in this area?
12. Observe as the meter shows you the percent of laughter energy you have in that moment, when your energy drops down to serious. Validate the truth of this experience for yourself! Then place that meter inside an imaginary bubble and pop it so it all dissolves.
13. Ask yourself: What am I afraid of losing if I allow myself to increase my inner humor in relation to this person or situation? Decide to effortlessly unmatch from that serious person or situation right now. Use the bubble popping activity to release energy (thoughts, emotions, pictures).
14. Ask yourself: How much inner laughter would I like to give myself in relation to this person or situation?
15. Give yourself permission to embody and experience as much inner laughter as you'd like in relation to this. Remember to

laugh or smile if you'd like; it will speed the process of unmatching from serious energy to engaging with laughter energy.

16. Ask a fresh laughter meter: Now how much inner laughter do I have? Watch the meter as it shows you the updated percent of inner laughter you now have in relation to that person or situation that you have just unmatched from. If your laughter increased in any amount, that's an extremely powerful start. You can continue to bump it up over time, even during your busy day.
17. Validate the truth of this experience for yourself. Then place the meter inside an imaginary bubble and pop it so it dissolves.
18. Use the Golden Sun activity (Activity 1, Chapter 1) to give yourself that renewed and updated quality of inner humor in present time. Fill yourself up with it. Observe where it goes. Congratulate yourself!
19. Note what transforms over time, perhaps by making an inner laugh graph!

Activity 2
Letting Go of Guilty Feelings

Feelings of guilt can keep us in serious energy. Here is an exercise to manage those feelings in a creative and intuitive way, that might even make you laugh. Shifting out of guilt energy fuels more creative power and allows you to embody much greater levels of self-care and harmony in your daily life.

Directions

1. Sit in a chair with your feet on the floor. Give yourself three conscious breaths.
2. Say *Hello* to your amazing body by joyfully saying, "I love you."
3. Greet yourself as the soul presence you are by validating your bright light and your power within. Say *Hello* to yourself! Quiet your analyzer by asking it to turn down the volume or intensity level to an optimized, balanced level for you in the present moment.

4. Be centered behind your eyes in your neutral awareness, in the present moment.
5. Ground yourself (Chapter 4, Activity 1). Set your energy in a high vibrational frequency, such as appreciation, joy, enthusiasm, abundance, humor, and/or playful curiosity, using the Golden Sun activity (Chapter 1, Activity 1).
6. Choose an inner, work-in-progress area where you have feelings of guilt that you'd like to heal and release so you can update to the present.
7. Imagine a gauge that is 0 to100 percent. Ask yourself how much guilt energy (100 percent is the highest) you are currently experiencing in relation to an area. Are you surprised? Dissolve or explode that gauge in a bubble.
8. Imagine a guilt-o-meter that is vertical, from 0 to 100 percent. Now imagine a gold, magnetic rose that gently brings down your guilt-o-meter (in relation to your chosen area) to as low as you like. Observe what that experience is like for you (i.e., feelings, colors, thoughts, etc.). You can bring this down to 0 percent anytime you like. Over time, this will shift your awareness around what makes you feel guilty, and help you reduce how often you match guilt energy in relationship to others. If you find it hard to bring down your imaginary guilt-o-meter, start popping bubbles (or roses) with thoughts, emotions, resistance energy, opinions, etc., so that you can have more fun and get more done!

Activity 3
Live Like a Laughter Leader

Remember the story about my daughter in the emergency room? This might sound funny, but it's true: Regardless of your role, position, or duties, you are always a leader when you consciously hold an energy vibration that is equally beneficial to yourself and others, such as compassion, neutrality, joy, collaboration, appreciation, and inner laughter, to name a few. These frequencies are not to be reserved for special occasions. That would be a serious mistake (ha ha). In this activity you will become intimate with your serious- and laughter-energy languages. You will gain clarity and discern the people, places, and situations where you tend to match either serious or laughter energies, to:

- give you a conscious choice about which energy you prefer in the moment and
- become faster and more adept at shifting into your inner laughter for greater intuitive responses, communication, adaptability, and resilience.

Directions

1. Sit in a chair with your feet on the floor. Give yourself three conscious breaths.
2. Say *Hello* to your amazing body by joyfully appreciating your relationship with it.
3. Greet yourself as the soul presence you are by validating your bright light and your power within. Say *Hello* to yourself! Quiet your analyzer by asking it to turn down the volume or intensity level to an optimized, balanced level for you in the present moment.
4. Be centered behind your eyes in your neutral awareness, in the present moment.
5. Ground yourself (Chapter 4, Activity 1). Set your energy in a high vibrational frequency, such as appreciation, joy, enthusiasm, humor, and/or playful curiosity, using the Golden Sun activity (Chapter 1, Activity 1).
6. Make a list of when, where, and in what ways you match with both the serious energy and laughter energy of colleagues, clients, patients, students, family members, friends, media, advertising, bosses, authority, institutions, organizations, etc.
7. Make a list of when, where, and in what ways others match *your* humorous state and serious state.
8. Make a list of all the activities that can increase your laughter meter. You could watch comedy, sing along to fun songs, read

inspiring books, or listen to podcasts that make you feel happy. Hang out with people who enjoy having a laugh or who are dynamic and interesting to engage with, or play with your dog, cat, child, or partner. Make a list of corny jokes and share them.

9. Using the Golden Sun activity (Activity 1, Chapter 1), fill yourself with golden suns full of inner laughter energy, every morning while you meditate, shower, exercise, walk your dog, or commute to work. The more challenging the day, the more you can saturate yourself to overflowing in this healing vibration.
10. Decide to lead with your inner laughter energy frequency when you encounter serious energies that are not serving you or others. Give others the opportunity to match your inner levity energy and uplift their lives and communities. It's a great way to pay it forward.
11. Practice engaging your inner laughter out in the world and see what happens.

Activity 4
Humor Hydration: Laughter Yoga

Laughter yoga is a great way to increase your laughter meter to shift out of the serious intellect and into the spaciousness of intuition, creativity, and imagination. This type of yoga engages voluntary laughter to provide similar physiological and psychological benefits as spontaneous laughter. It combines laughter with yoga breathing techniques (pranayama) that bring more oxygen to the body and brain. You may start out with an obligatory laugh, but you'll soon be laughing for real. For more information, watch laughter yoga videos on social media or YouTube. Start with intuitive tools and incorporate laughter yoga at step 6 in the directions below.

Directions

1. Sit in a chair with your feet on the floor. Give yourself three conscious breaths.

2. Say *Hello* to your amazing body by joyfully appreciating your communication with it.
3. Greet yourself as the soul presence you are by validating your bright light and your power within.
4. Say *Hello* to yourself! Quiet your analyzer by asking it to turn down the volume or intensity level to an optimized, balanced level for you in the present moment.
5. Be centered behind your eyes in your neutral awareness, in the present moment.
6. Ground yourself (Chapter 4, Activity 1). Set your energy in a high vibrational frequency, such as appreciation, joy, abundance, enthusiasm, humor, and/or playful curiosity, using the Golden Sun activity (Chapter 1, Activity 1). Now get ready for laughter yoga!
7. Breathe in deeply, breathe out slowly, and laugh!
8. Breathe in deeply, breathe out slowly, and laugh!
9. That was easy! Repeat until you are overflowing with laughter!
10. Use the Golden Sun activity (Activity 1, Chapter 1) to give yourself laughter energy and any other supportive qualities with which you'd like to refresh. Fill yourself up with these qualities. With your awareness, notice where it goes in your body and space. Celebrate!

Activity 5
Humor Hydration: Star in Your Own Comedy Show

One of the most powerful ways to release a bookmarked picture is through laughter, enthusiasm, or an inner smile. Anytime you increase your energetic frequency through levity, you transform your inner landscape into a more flexible canvas in which to do your inner creative work of healing. After all, these pictures aren't the fault of anyone, so you might as well laugh at them! This activity will help you become a humorous observer of your pictures. Because intuition connects you with limitless inner creative power, you will use your imagination as if you are the director of your own sitcom or comedy movie to release old, low-frequency patterns. Ready? And… action!

Directions

1. Sit in a chair with your feet on the floor. Give yourself three conscious breaths.
2. Say *Hello* to your amazing body by saying, "I love you as you are."
3. Greet yourself as the soul presence you are by validating your bright light and your power within. Say *Hello* to yourself! Quiet your analyzer by asking it to turn down the volume or intensity level to an optimized, balanced level for you in the present moment.
4. Be centered behind your eyes in your neutral awareness, in the present moment.
5. Ground yourself (Chapter 4, Activity 1) and set your energy in a high vibrational frequency, such as appreciation, joy, enthusiasm, humor, and/or playful curiosity, using the Golden Sun activity (Chapter 1, Activity 1).
6. Imagine a giant movie screen in front of you. Choose a situation or relationship that currently feels challenged or hard.
7. Ask yourself: If I were directing a comedy version of this situation or relationship, how would I reframe this scene, to be as funny as possible?
8. Visualize the entire situation or relationship as your favorite comedy, imagining each conversation, action, expression, or next step within a comedy framework. Imagine each interaction in a new energy of ever-increasing creativity.
9. Fill the entire scene with golden suns full of inner-laughter, energy frequency.
10. Place any images that are serious into a bubble and pop the bubble so everything evaporates. Return your attention to the unfolding comedy. Don't forget to smile and/or laugh!

11. Practice this as many times as you need, until you are rewriting your script into a new experience of high-frequency energies of creativity, playfulness, abundance, love, gratitude, and joy.

Chapter Seven
Be the Conscious Creative Director of Your Life

Setting My Sights with Nosey the Pony

When you were a child or teen, did you ever have someone tell you (verbally, nonverbally, or with body language): "Don't do that" or "Don't look at that"? Did you immediately imagine seeing yourself doing or looking at whatever *that* was? It's pretty hard not to imagine it, isn't it? If it was something nonbeneficial, it doesn't matter at all that you imagined it, it just matters if you followed it out or got stuck in it. The story below illustrates how you can unconsciously get stuck putting energy into a direction you don't actually wish to experience. The clearer you are about what you'd like to envision—from nonresistance or from conscious awareness—the easier it is to set your sights on where you're going, without as many detours.

A little Shetland pony named Nosey taught me the importance of setting my sights to consciously direct my life. When I was nine years old, I took jumping lessons. The first thing Nosey taught me was to set my line of vision exactly where I wanted to end up. Both physically and intuitively, where you look is generally where you go.

As Nosey and I trotted toward the jump, the first thing I did was let my fear distract me. I'd been told, "Don't look down," when approaching a jump. So, I had already imagined looking down, many times before I even got in the saddle. The information about not looking down was useful except that I made it the main focus of my energy.

I looked straight down, exactly where I was afraid of falling, and automatically imagined falling. As a result, my nervous system engaged with that fear energy. I then unconsciously tensed my body, which caused me to slightly pull back on the reins. This sent a very mixed message to Nosey, who hit her brakes right in front of the jump. I fell off, and Nosey happily wandered off to graze. This was one way to ground myself. Just not the easiest way! Unmanaged images of fear can temporarily unground us. Grounded space creates stability and presence from which to set your sights on your next aligned choice or decision. Trust your intuitive sight to know whether the choices ahead offer a beneficial direction for your purposes and positive growth.

Take two. I imagined easily clearing the jump, setting my sights exactly where I would land. I consciously changed my energy, and my nervous system received the message and calmed. I relaxed my hands on the reins as we approached the jump. Together, as a team, we gracefully sailed over the small jump. I felt like a champion rider (although for anyone who knows how little a Shetland pony is, the image should make you laugh).

The Unity of Your Soul-Body Team

Are you willing to explore, discover, heal, or redefine those unconscious patterns that have run your show, and give yourself permission to receive and create intuitively? If your answer is *yes*, then you are ready to consciously direct your life as a soul-body team.

It is through your grounded, intuitive awareness that you as the soul and body team consciously show up in unity, to create together from the whole of life. This means accessing all the qualities and capabilities of *you* that are your birthright but have been underutilized. Many people don't consciously know they are a team. Simply recognizing the unity of your soul presence and body is powerful.

There's collaboration in this unity because you are neither split into two separate halves moving in parallel but disconnected dances nor looking down while trying to clear a hurdle! If you (as your soul presence) seek inner growth, but you (as your body) obsess over playing (metaphorical) slot machines, things can get murky pretty fast. As your body heads for the casino, your bright presence tries to register for a meditation class. Or if you (as a conscious, creative being) seek wellness, but you (as the body) just want to scroll through your phone on the couch, things can feel frustrating. The intellect culture roots for the side of the metaphorical slot machines because there's no validation for spiritual growth and consciousness. This divisiveness can leave you feeling confused, or swinging back and forth like a pendulum, rather than finding your balanced sweet spot.

To optimize this unity, it helps to check in with your inner permission meter and see where you have unconsciously set limits on your creativity, inner trust, clear seeing, growth, and awareness. Then, discern where you are actually looking, both internally and with your eyes. Are you looking toward the completion of purposeful goals and dreams, or are you looking anywhere else, in fear, guilt, or doubt, led by your distracted body?

There is little difference between my pony experience and your soul-body experience. When you, as a grounded soul presence, look from your awareness at where you wish to go, your body will follow, and together you will reach your preferred destination. True, your body might act like an opinionated but lovely Shetland pony who doesn't like jumping. Or perhaps your body is more like a steady Morgan horse who will stay right with you or a giant Percheron draft horse doing the heavy pulling. Maybe your body is like a horse that loves to race but needs a lot of training, so you don't get thrown off at high speed or end up where you didn't plan to go. Loving, accepting, and valuing your "body personality" as it is greatly enhances your team's ability to innovatively and consciously direct your life.

> ***Setting your sights for your life path or next steps is greatly supported when you have a conscious relationship as a soul-body team.***

An embodied experience of the wise, aware soul presence collaborating with intellect, feelings, senses, inner knowing, and creativity in your everyday life, will support you every step of the way, if you allow it!

Maddy's Story: Setting Her Sights on Unity

Maddy, a talented elementary school teacher with children of her own, registered for an intuitive tools class. Her goals for the class were to learn how to consciously ground and handle stress in a more creative way, especially in relation to managing the chaotic energy at school. She was also interested in learning how to set her energy for smoother transitions from work to home. Two weeks before class started, several family events conflicted with the class. She felt guilty missing the family events, so she canceled joining the class. She had gotten divorced and felt guilty about that too. Maddy often unconsciously set her sights on feeling guilty and responsible, stemming from old pictures from her female lineage. This overthinking pattern limited her from making choices to support her personal growth, and happiness.

During her daughter's basketball game, Maddy felt resentful for giving up her class, because it was intended to support her all-around well-being. This was another common pattern for Maddy—feeling conflicted between two directions and never feeling contented with either choice. She'd make a choice, but not *fully* choose it, because half her awareness was split into an alternative. Neither choice had her full attention, power, or creativity. She felt like her bright presence had registered for class, but her body personality was sitting at the game.

Maddy gave herself a quiet pause and in that space realized how important the intuitive tools class was for her. She knew the benefits of the class would ripple out to her family and her students at school. Perhaps taking the class would even model for her daughter or students the benefits of nurturing oneself.

The next time the class was offered, she registered immediately and decided it was a much-needed inner commitment to shift her line of sight from guilt to self-care, out of limitations. Without realizing it,

Maddy was already practicing conscious soul-body skills. Almost immediately, Maddy experienced a delightful aha moment, because she saw how this promise to herself created space and permission for her spiritual growth. The first time, Maddy only mentally registered for the class; she didn't really *register* on a soul-body team level in terms of creating a space for it in her busy life. This time, Team Maddy was all in! She immediately recognized how this was enormously applicable to other arenas of her life. In some areas, it was natural or innate for her to give herself the space to achieve her goals, but with her writing, not so much. For years she had wanted to write a book, but because she had not created the receptive space for it, it stayed in her thinking space, on a mental to-do list. Her runway was cluttered with reasons (pictures) that kept her from taking off or landing this particular desired project. This awareness was transformative.

During the class, Maddy experienced a cascade of illuminating aha moments. She gained clarity about some of her responsibility pictures around being a "perfect" mom, resulting in over-giving, feeling responsible for everything, and yes, guilty too! For example, she often overcorrected, like with a scratch, instead of putting on just one bandage, she'd put on three. She had often felt that she alone was the only one who could solve her kids' problems, yet this pattern of worrying was stressful, and perhaps was blocking support from arriving where it was most needed. Every time she engaged in fun projects, she felt so much less worried about little things that couldn't be controlled or fixed.

These realizations gave Maddy new insights about her career as a teacher and the ways she had set her sights on overworking in this arena as well. She recognized how her attitude toward over-giving at work had even caused a few colleagues to hand her their duties; because she seemed so willing to do everything, they mistakenly thought she had more time than they did. Once again, she'd been providing three bandages where only one was needed! Her intuition was there to discern how many bandages were needed, but guilt (showing up as responsibility) had been directing her. Both in her personal and professional lives, Maddy had been looking directly at burnout. She began to consciously reframe her sights with her vast creative power, necessary for her to find joy, harmony, and self-care in all areas of her life.

Maddy recalled how her kind parents did not give themselves time or space for their own inner development and well-being, even though they were extremely giving in the world. In her family, the idea of self-care was a foreign language. Isn't that stuff just for wimpy or whiny people? Those were their pictures. Without conscious access to their higher awareness, her parents couldn't fully see the value of the difference they made in the world around them. Instead, they always felt they hadn't made *enough* difference, so they just worked harder being healers to everyone, until their bodies were worn out.

Maddy shifted out of her family's limiting patterns as she practiced a new language defined by her soul-body teamwork, applying grounding and affirming her inner guidance while on the go. Before, Maddy thought she could either support her body or support her soul presence, which is why she felt so divided between two directions all the time. Now she felt free to integrate herself in a more unified way, living from the wholeness of her life.

Asking Questions, Finding Answers

When the body is in charge, the overthinking intellect boxes you in, based on old picture patterns. The antidote is curiosity mixed with enthusiasm to explore your spiritual landscape. One way is to start by asking yourself questions that enhance your growth and bring you deeper into your limitless awareness. The very act of asking questions and releasing pictures brings you into the light of consciousness, so your old patterns cannot run you on their unconscious hamster wheel without your permission any longer!

Exploring your authentic questions from appreciation, curiosity, self-discovery, and value begins the journey toward heartfelt, loving questions that result in greater inner freedom. As you ask these questions, continue to find your inner laughter. Remember, where you look is where you go. Set your sights from a place of clear seeing!

During many years of teaching, I have noticed that people often have an inner question that is quite different from what their outer question is. That's why my goal is always to help them find their own answers, as well as their authentic questions.

Getting to the heart of your own questions is an invitation, an interview, a dance, a harvest, and an orchestration. It's an application of imagination and creativity. From that center, the possibilities of your inner expansion, away from old limitations radiate. With practice, you will learn to ask questions that are true and correct for you. Once you spot them, the questions you ask will help you to know yourself more fully as you dissolve the pictures and open to seeing new potentials. This practice begins with your own deepest and simplest questions, addressed to the intuitive, infinite, powerful, imaginative you.

> *Intuitive-based questions that are addressed to you as the bright light you are, will always point you in a direction that naturally benefits you and the greater good.*

By following your intuitive guidance your answers can fulfill your aspirations and improve the conditions around you in ways that you may or may not notice but can trust are there. Once you practice, you will find that asking your questions and discovering your answers helps you to refine and redefine your next steps and your growth.

A Yard Sale of Questions, Not All Are a Good Deal

In your everyday life, it can be a fun practice to notice the difference between asking a question that engages your growth, healing, and inner knowing, and asking a question that is not authentically yours. In our families, educational systems, professions, and society, we get plenty of practice asking questions that are not our own. These questions are extremely valuable too. However, asking questions that are aligned and specific for you, and the information you are seeking, brings you to delightful transformation and expansion. Knowing what kind of knowledge you are seeking is an excellent starting point for asking questions. Are you seeking intellectual knowledge or intuitive knowledge? In a day, there is plenty of space for both. But without recognizing the difference, your search can get subtly jumbled.

Become aware of how intellect questions, based on outside information, keep you from asking your intuitive questions, based on inner information. Observe the content of the question and curiously investigate its origins. Are you asking the same questions your well-meaning father asked you when he wanted you to hurry up for school, stop being so messy, or choose better friends? Are you asking questions about money or self-confidence that are really questions your loving mom asked herself, and you think they personally belong to you? Maybe just reframing those questions from your own energy is a game changer for you. What if you're seeking courage, and you keep getting fearful answers? Perhaps it is because the questions you're asking are mostly absorbed from those around you. Maybe you are asking a fantastic question that your mother or father asked because they looked at the world with gratitude, enthusiasm, curiosity, generosity, equanimity, creativity, courage, or adaptability, and you matched that energy. If that's true for you, *Yay for you!* Probably it's a little of both.

Letting go of some outdated questions makes a space for something more relevant to you in the present. Revising your questions streamlines them for clarity. Offer yourself some laughter therapy, ground yourself, access your imagination, and then ask the question from that limitless place within you. Once you shift your question into a more intuitive format, answers come more easily, and you take a quantum leap in awareness and inner freedom.

Interviewing Yourself with Spacious Patience

Like all good interviewers know, conducting an interview requires good listening skills. If you ask a question and demand an immediate response without any pause, this lack of patience forces the pace of the interview and you might receive discombobulated, partial, or no answers in response. The same principle applies to asking and receiving in relationship with your intuition. When you are grounded, your analyzer is quieted from overthinking debris, and you have set your energy space in supportive qualities, you have created space to receive and explore clear insights.

When you're the intuitive interviewer, there's a balance between knowing some of your questions ahead of time yet not getting stuck on them in a way that creates expectations, rigidity, or formulaic outcomes. Understanding the greater purpose of your inner interview questions ahead of time helps you to streamline and focus your results. You will direct your inner communication into an area highlighted for exploration and relevant for the context of what you are seeking. Once again, this is a process of setting your sights. Many times, I intuitively see people ask a question but just under the surface of their awareness they have already decided what the answer *should* be. I will humorously call this intuitive repellent. Another intuitive repellent is making an assumption ahead of time that is stuck in your mind and creates a locked door against new discoveries.

Simultaneously, you'll maximize your self-interview by pausing often to create an opening through which something broader than your questions might arrive. In energetic terms, this gives space for the answer to birth itself in a creative way. A question may lead you into an unexplored area, revealing a new question, suddenly drawing your attention in a different way. Set your sights on establishing an energy space for your interview with qualities such as spaciousness, patience, abundance, and joy, imagining a clear outcome, or other qualities that support your intentions.

> ***Pay attention to how quickly the ungrounded, overthinking mind wants to start chattering as soon as you've asked a question!***

Your attention might travel from your original question toward a bookmarked picture that is indirectly connected to the original question. There could be many tangents that quickly devolve your interview process into a tangled mess. If this happens (and it will!), don't worry and don't match that serious energy. Patiently reground and return to your original question, because you're in charge here; you're the boss!

Questions Divisive to Soul-Body Teamwork

Some questions from the intellect simply may go unanswered and require reformatting. Don't play go-fetch with survival or prove-it pictures, when after all, *Hello* they're just pictures directing your attention! Choose your inner questions with kindness and self-respect.

Some questions will split your soul and body team from your unified power by invalidating you. You silently, unconsciously ask yourself these questions. They almost never show up formed and succinct, or they would be easy to spot with rational responses. They sneak into your internal conversation because they have lived with you your whole life, hiding in plain sight.

One example is when a person uses their unconscious awareness to gauge whether it's safe to speak their truth or be fully themselves in a group of people. Yet it's not uncommon to be in a group of people where one person would prefer to dominate the group if possible and not have people speak their truth. No good comes from obeying that unconscious directive with your unconscious intuition. With unconscious intuition, you are intuitively reading and matching the energy, without discerning what's really your energy. So, then you might also form questions that are not your own. Once you realize this, you might change: "Is it safe to speak?" to, "What is the highest good way to communicate my truth that this group of people can hear?"

Invalidating questions can arise from bookmarked pictures of perfection. For example, "Am I good enough?" is not a validating question. It's a trick question!

> *You cannot feel invalidated in any area of your life, feelings, or thoughts unless a part of your creative energy is trapped in a picture that tells you that you have to be perfect.*

Perfectionism might serve you well in a specific area such as certain types of professions. Yet in other areas of your life, where you have a lot of perfectionistic patterns, you can become susceptible to the opinions, agendas, or directives that tell you the most perfect way you have to do something, or create, or live. Advertising and social media are great examples; we are literally bombarded with images of "perfect."

This can cause you to unconsciously ask invalidating, comparison questions which match serious, low vibrational energy. Your inner knowing opens your awareness so that you can prioritize where to put your creative energy. That way, you are not putting your creative power into "perfect" within areas of your life that don't require such high levels of perfection. When you do this, it can waste time that could be applied elsewhere for greater benefit. When you recognize that your most aligned way is to create from your own energy, not from those images, you become more neutral.

Validate your bright awareness and say, "That's just a picture, that's not something I need to act on or be directed by." Say *Hello* to your laughter, and simply move on rather than dwell in it.

Invalidating questions don't take you directly to the answers you seek. Keep in mind, though, that they *do* guide you to where you are ready to heal. With practice you will appreciate that no question needs to split your soul-body team.

Rose's Relationship Questions

Rose had a fulfilling career working for a nonprofit that helped children. She was also an incredible artist, when she had time here and there to create art and poetry. Rose identified as a "big healer," and serving this way allowed her to focus her creative energy to assist lots of children and their community, too. This left her with little time for finding a life partner. Each time she started a relationship, it ended up being the same type of person, just dressed differently. Yet these realizations always took her by surprise, as if she was blindsided each time. This was especially annoying because she was extremely good at applying her inner guidance in many other areas of her life, with incredible outcomes. She used her intuition to find an affordable house that she liked, travel to unusual places, apply for work-related grants to help the children, and to make new friendships that were nourishing.

Her potential partners all seemed to track positively in the beginning, having qualities and goals she admired, and having interests she shared. Eventually, these potential life partners turned out to be "projects" instead of reciprocal, loving relationships.

Rose often asked, "Why can't I meet the right person? How is it that I can't find a good match? Is there something wrong with me?" These invalidating questions limited the answers she sought. In this area, Rose expended a lot of energy in a frustrated space of wanting. At first, she didn't realize that she could change her inner questions. When she discerned the difference between her intellect and inner knowing and the way pictures impacted the questions she was asking, she gained more insight. Wanting (as unconscious, frustrated energy) was closing down her inner receiving space in this area. As she continued practicing intuitive tools, all that growth (healing) caused a lot of pictures to leave her space, and suddenly she was having a new experience in her awareness. It was like turning on a light in a dark room that had always been there in her house and seeing what was there, in a neutral way.

A formerly unconscious question came to the surface of her mind. "How can I fix this person perfectly so they can be more like me?" The question surprised her and made her laugh. Intellectually, she knew the, "How can I fix this person?" part of her question already. "So they can be more like me" was not something she had been aware of, yet it resonated with her. She did find it humorously ironic, since as an artist she fully supported everyone being uniquely themselves! Soon, Rose was aware of another subtle question. "How can I figure out what's wrong with this person so we can be in a relationship?" Rose observed how this was a trick question, because everyone has faults, and if the whole focus is to figure out what's wrong with a person to then make them be more like her, that's all she would get.

Yet on the other side of the pendulum swing, if she is not clearly discerning from her inner guidance what romantic match is healthy and aligned for her, she is equally off-kilter. *Hello* balance!

The energy of Rose's questions didn't validate her true desires, and she realized that it had all started with trying to heal the relationship between her father and mother, as a child. Her old questions unconsciously bounced around like pinballs, taking up space, leaving no room for her to receive her true questions. Rose discovered how her "responsibility pictures" fixated her attention as a big healer on self-imposed goals of "perfectly" fixing someone. There were also unconscious "failure pictures" in her space because she had not been able to fully heal the relationship between her parents, even though this was not her responsibility. She'd been using her unconscious intuition to tune into energy patterns in a possible mate that matched this. Then she'd hit the failure pictures again when she couldn't heal her potential mate.

As Rose began to play with her creativity, she had fun writing new questions for herself, as poems. She began to attract a different kind of partner, from a space that combined clear discernment with acceptance of imperfections. Acceptance allowed her to stop focusing on fixing, which had been pushing away her love interests because they felt controlled, or it attracted them because they wanted a caretaker rather than a reciprocal relationship. She began to see that she had not failed as a big healer at all. Rose noted everywhere in her life (such as her profession) where she was already authentically engaged in positive expressions of her healing abilities. She then realized she needed to find even more healthy outlets for her many forms of creative expression, that were all healing. This diversification of her creative focus helped her feel more excited about life and naturally backed her off from putting so much effort into finding a relationship. She had so much overflowing healing energy that it was important for her to guide it into as many forms of expression as possible and balance it with plenty of space to receive.

This change of energy and awareness created a new level of inner permission for Rose to choose and allow a partner who nurtured her. Her most aligned match turned out to be someone she had known for two years through her shared group of friends but had not been drawn to romantically. Yet once she went on a few dates, with her new outlook she realized this person was deeply attractive to her: physically, emotionally, and spiritually.

True Questions Overcome Limitations of Bookmarked Picture Patterns

As you can see, a good way to discover your own true questions is through first discovering the questions you absorbed and carried from your inherited and lived patterns. Exploring questions shines a light on the unconscious limitations imposed by these patterns and brings them into your consciousness so your soul-body team can update them. Many times, your absorbed questions show up as intellectual statements of "fact" like, "You aren't good at that." "You aren't the type of person that knows how to do that well." You may have unintentionally subscribed to a statement in sixth grade that in present time is completely obsolete but still subtly limits your approach in one area of your life.

Limitations are ways that your creative energy gets detoured or filtered into pictures (as energy, emotions, thoughts) that drop you down into a rigid rut like: "You have to be perfect," or "You need to be the smartest to survive," or the most stoic or emotional to survive, the busiest, safest, wildest, the most conservative or the most in control, best at sports, best at making money, the best looking, or accomplished in some unattainable way that never, ever is enough. Releasing pictures clears patterns or limits absorbed from your family, lineage, society, school, professional training, culture, peers, partners, media, and institutions to which you unconsciously subscribed as the most "real." Asking your true questions is a route to healing your intuitive biome.

These kinds of limiting pictures that form invalidating questions present themselves through your subtle reactions, thoughts, and emotions in unexpected ways because they have been part of your space for so long, yet not truly your energy. They may even help you in one area, but they always cause an imbalance in an area of your life where you struggle or seek to grow. Your intuitive awareness helps you move from your intellectual understanding of what questions you absorbed, to an experiential release of those questions. The result is a new space of clarity within your mind that can also rewire your nervous system. Changing your mind is easier when you first change your energy (release the bookmarked patterns). When you shift your energy, it's much easier to transform your thoughts, feelings, and questions. This starts with giving yourself permission for a new experience, framework, or outcome. Having an honest laugh with yourself greatly supports this! Even better, have an honest laugh with a trusted friend, family member, or partner! Studies show that being vulnerable actually strengthens relationships.

There are times when what you set your sights on, despite your inner work, remains frustratingly unattainable. A dream or goal that's truly orchestrated for you may stay out of your reach because the timing hasn't yet arrived. Other times, you discover later that it truly wasn't the most orchestrated direction for you to go because what you initially envisioned was not really part of your greater purpose. This can be an extremely validating realization, but you have to trust your well-practiced intuition and life wisdom as part of this flow because the realizations come as hindsight!

Once you've cleared some limits, don't forget to immediately celebrate. Yay for you! Yay for everyone, because you also free up others when you release a picture, since, like mycelia, we're all interconnected. But don't stop there, because while clearing out the old is essential to make a free space for your next steps, it doesn't in and of itself create something new. As the conscious creative director of your life, you are responsible for that part too.

Jack's Story: A Self-Permission Slip to Let Go of Limitations and Create Anew

Jack was seventeen and en route to being a talented visual artist. He was extremely capable, but highly self-critical. This was not the type of critical feedback that helps with discerning what needs improvement and thoughtfully implementing it because he had plenty of that quality and skill. This was a limiting pattern installed in his childhood, which hung out in the back of his mind and invalidated him for not being good enough.

For example, when Jack created a piece of art that would go on the school wall at arts night, although adults and friends would give incredible compliments, all he could see were the faults of his creation. In his mind's eye he'd visualize the work of a famous artist and compare his art to that person. Other times he'd listen to inner questions that invalidated him to his core, spiraling him into a set of hopeless emotions about his future as an artist. Jack was aware how those low emotions made him feel, but he was unsure about how to get himself out of this stuck groove. His emotions also overflowed into self-criticisms about the attractiveness of his body and personality traits.

Jack was aware of being intuitive and sensitive, but over the years it was often hard to distinguish what he absorbed from outside energy and what was his true creative energy. Some days he'd feel enthusiastic and positive about his art, and other days his self-confidence crashed and burned. Because each creation was unique to his own style of creativity, ultimately there was no way to gauge ahead of time what would be received well by the public. As a visual artist it was pretty easy to visualize what thoughts were floating around his consciousness. Some days these critical thoughts seemed like a depository of theoretical, hypothetical, critical, and analytical feedback that was uninvited. Sometimes he wondered, *How do we know what is really us?*

Jack's invalidating questions asked, "Am I good enough to do this, or am I just kidding myself?" or "Do I have any talent at all?" Other times, the questions and pictures showed up more like commentary from an outer, male authority, saying, "People are just being nice about your art, because they don't want to hurt your feelings. Why don't you get real?" Intuitively, Jack knew these criticisms weren't really his true voice, but how could he stop them? He knew that some of his friends carried the same invalidating types of subtle questions and pictures in their own areas of interest. They used survival coping mechanisms to override or numb their feelings, like staying super busy with no time to pause, smoking a lot of weed, drinking, or drugging, or becoming overachievers or underachievers, each on a pendulum swing. He was compassionate to why they did this, but he didn't want to numb his awareness. He knew engaging in these activities would shut down some of his creativity and his joy of life. He had set his sights on balance, awareness, creative expression, and manifesting his goals in the world. A part of him was aware that as long as he could imagine and envision, he could get there. Even though he didn't have the money to get there, over and over he quietly imagined visiting New York City and being an artist. Not *becoming* an artist, in future time. *Being* an artist in present time. He could feel this dream in his body as real.

One day, feeling low, Jack confided in his most grounded and stable friend. He told her how crappy he really felt about his art, and how, at the same time, he aspired to go to art school and pursue his dream. He was afraid she'd judge him, so it felt risky to admit this to her.

To his surprise, rather than judge him, Jack's friend taught him some strategies she'd learned in a private, intuitive tools session. She shared with him that she had observed how often she unconsciously matched the energy of classmate drama at school. Then she would find herself sucked into it as a mediator, which made her feel overwhelmed. She realized that she could be conscious about not matching that energy, and this changed her relationships in a positive way, without any talking.

She gave Jack an intuitive assignment to do a little inner exploring. She told him to close his eyes and tap into his imagination (that was easy!). When he recognized naysayer questions that began with, "I want…" "Why can't I…" and "How can I…" not to mention, "I suck, because…" his first task was to ground himself and find some inner laughter, release those pictures into bubbles and pop them, and reset his energy with golden suns full of qualities of what he would like to experience instead. His second assignment was to change the trajectory of those questions by creating new ones that would set his sights so that he would clear any hurdles and land in a place that was on his path.

Jack created many fresh questions in his mind (and on paper). One of them was, "I'm ready to become more aware and skilled as an artist. What is the next step for my highest growth?" Jack's friend showed him how to visualize a permission meter that represented all the qualities he already had available within. He had been in a rut thinking that everything was somehow "out there," and he had to go fetch it, so recognizing what was within himself was a little different. This didn't mean there wasn't plenty of work needed to get where he envisioned. He felt like he was now "senior" within his body, directing his own journey. This made him laugh because in his family he had been referred to as junior, and he had received a whole lot of directives down his male lineage about how to create your life the manly way. Anything that made Jack laugh changed his energy in an instant, so this was all a good first step!

> ***Being intuitive is the ability to make a simple decision that's orchestrated for you.***

In that moment, Jack made a new decision that really settled in his bones and soul. This didn't mean he was never going to hear that self-critical voice barking untrue directives or invalidating questions again. That voice was always going to try to get one by, on occasion. Now when an invalidating question or directive popped up, Jack knew how to say *Hello* to it, and actively reformat the question to lead him to his vast inner knowing and powerful creative expression. He made a conscious choice to lead with his pure and simple awareness, instead of buying into every emotion that paraded through his mind. Once he did that he began to tap into his true feelings, which often guided him with expressing his art. Feeling his own authentic feelings was also supporting him in manifesting his goal.

Soon after he changed his energy relationship to his questions, a kind teacher at his school said *Hello* to Jack's creativity, validated his artistic skills, and told Jack about an upcoming art contest. He entered the contest and won first prize, an all-expenses-paid trip to New York

City. Jack now attends an art college on scholarship. The support of his friend's intuitive tools, plus his teacher's thoughtful guidance that led to winning the prize, helped Jack give himself 100 percent permission to imagine his next steps. And his imagination became his reality.

Freeing Your Creative Power

To change, you must create something new within yourself, adapting a new quality of life. For example, when you release the energy of resentment, it opens the doors to create more inner laughter, generosity, or peace in your life. When you release fear, you might choose to create self-love as a quality in your mind. When you let go of rejection, set your sights on appreciation or self-acceptance. You have the creative power, backed by your soul-body team, to set your sights anywhere.

When your creative power dwells for too long in perfectionistic or critical pictures, you may feel like you live in a narrow corridor. Then you tap on the wall, and realize it's just a cheap cubicle, a house of cards. As it topples, revealing wide-open space, you might immediately launch yourself forward in a joyful dance. Or you might stay where you are for a little while, unsure about your next steps to find expression in the vast creative space now available. All that open space is exciting yet can be overwhelming at first! That's a lovely moment to just pause, observe, and receive.

Many people lament their perceived lack of access to creativity. Now that you see below surface appearances, it's easy to understand how this can seem so real. Here is a worthwhile question: Have you made space (as energy) for your creative expression in this world? If you wish to look a little deeper, create a gauge from 0 to 100 percent, and check in with your permission levels. There's always time for a redo. Your creative expression is not limited to one category, it's boundless. Envision a new receptive space to support your next steps.

How about this question: Are you unconsciously matching some energy that you'd like to unmatch from so that you can create a redo in some area that's ripe for a reset? That energy is in the past, and you are aiming to create from the present. What energy would you love to match that brings you joy in this moment? You have this energy within yourself, too! If it didn't already exist within you, you wouldn't know to seek it.

For me, when I maintain a consistent relationship with my writing and teaching, it seems the world around me begins to transform in subtle ways. Relationships shift without effort and my enthusiasm and joy amplify. I laugh more, feel fulfilled, forgive more easily, and am a more dynamic parent, friend, and family member. When I communicate through these channels of creative expression, a bigger space "suddenly" emerges for me, on all levels. More space also means greater relationship within my spiritual ecosystem. Each creative expression expands into another action guided by my inner knowing, so that it's purposeful rather than random. It's a feeling of being at home in my body, wherever I am.

The moment you decide to change your energy and forge a new way forward, you begin to share and simultaneously fulfill your purpose. This is your power in action. Writing or teaching definitely isn't for everyone. Each person has their unique areas of expression and purpose, for example singing, science, architecture, art, activism, medicine, psychology, coaching, mathematics, cooking, building a business, sailing, farming, parenting, gardening, and public speaking to name a few. Whatever it is, it has to be something that changes your energy in a way that improves the condition of your life. You might know it by the way it makes you feel and respond to the world around you.

> ***Can you give yourself a permission slip, signed by you as a soul presence in your incredible body, to start living more of your creative self-expression and purpose?***

If you are still a bit unsure of how to begin, ask an insightful question of yourself! Instead of allowing your unconscious to ask invalidating questions, consciously ask a question beginning with the word, *what*.

How is okay, but it can more easily end up as an intellect-based question. While *How do I...?* is fabulous for fixing a computer, car, or a broken bone, when it comes to you, asking *how* puts your intuition in the spin cycle of the overanalyzing mind.

For example, consider the following questions: "What do I already have within myself that I can offer the world or my community?" "What am I already sharing and expressing that I haven't fully recognized?" "What approach will support the next step of sharing my gifts, skills, creativity, healing, communication?" "What next steps will support me in exploring, enjoying, and expressing my passion or hobby?" "What might transform in my relationships in the world around me, and in the world within me, when I'm expressing from my authentic creative power?" "What actions will engage my authentic power as a soul-body team?" "What actions will allow me to discover or fulfill my purposes?" "What would I like to restore within myself that fills me with purpose or joy, inspires my creativity, helps me grow, or makes me feel a sense of awe and wonder?" Postulate that you know the answer and ask it to come through within a short period of time. Perhaps you'd enjoy asking this question: "What am I not fully seeing that I can appreciate that is right in front of me?" Maybe you will become aware of a new quality that is quietly blossoming within you as a result of your simple questions, addressed to the infinite you. Or you could look in the mirror and appreciate yourself exactly as you are.

Each time you receive a valuable answer that guides you in a purposeful flow, don't just move on immediately, pause for a few moments to fully receive it within your heart, mind, and soul. Allow the energy of your answer to be lovingly welcomed within you, your body, and your five senses. Be generous with yourself and give it space to grow in your inner biome!

Each time you reach a milestone with creating, do you automatically squash, undervalue, or invalidate your creation? Or do you immediately start worrying about what's next? When this happens, heal yourself through releasing some long-held pictures, and bring yourself happily into the present moment. Give yourself space to appreciate the fruits of your creation in present time. Whether you just organized a party for someone you love, finished a song or book, started your ideal job, opened your new business, healed or changed your life, or accomplished a goal or dream that you have envisioned for years, you put your heart, mind, and soul into creating something of value to share. Allow your creation to breathe and blossom with spacious orchestration from the wholeness of life. Imagine yourself standing in the golden glow of your creation and say *Hello* to your limitless intuitive creativity!

Intuitive Tools

Activity 1
The Vibrational Frequency of Giving

Vibrationally speaking, wanting something is like a closed hand offering no space to receive. Try wanting kindness, wanting a breath, or wanting a laugh. Now try giving yourself permission to receive kindness, a breath, or a laugh, with your open hand. See the difference? It's a different vibrational frequency, isn't it? A conscious decision to give yourself permission to receive is a clear signal that aligns your soul-body team in the direction of your sights. Notice how receptive and spacious it feels to give kindness within yourself as compared to wanting kindness. In this activity, you will set your sights on giving yourself permission to:

- make a daily decision that you are worth receiving with an open hand and
- increase your inner givingness and inner receiving.

Directions

1. Sit in a chair with your feet on the floor. Give yourself three conscious breaths.
2. Say *Hello* to your amazing body by joyfully appreciating all the ways it is a vessel for your creative expression in the world.
3. Greet yourself as the soul presence you are by validating your bright light and your power within. Say *Hello* to yourself! Quiet your analyzer by asking it to turn down the volume or intensity

level to an optimized, balanced level for you in the present moment.
4. Be centered behind your eyes in your neutral awareness, in the present moment.
5. Ground yourself (Chapter 4, Activity 1). Set your energy in a high vibrational frequency, such as appreciation, joy, enthusiasm, humor, and/or playful curiosity, using the Golden Sun activity (Chapter 1, Activity 1).
6. Open hand ("givingness"): What would you like to have, create, or share more of in the energy of infinite abundance? Choose a quality you seek to receive or give such as supportive spiritual or emotional growth, deeper friendships, easier communication with others, better relationships, feeling seen, more fun or laughter, more time, space or support for a creative project, improved well-being or health. Consider what the purpose of your desire relates to, like a garden to grow healthy food, money for a class or for financial stability, easier life organization flow so you have time for doing work, art, or play that you love. Clarifying your purpose greatly helps you recognize what is most valuable for you and your life versus what is extraneous to your unique purposes.
7. Decide to give to yourself. Say *Hello* to your inner givingness! Don't forget to pop bubbles as anything outdated rises to the surface when you put your attention on this area.
8. On an imaginary scale of 0 to 100 percent (imagine a gauge) what is your inner givingness at this moment?
9. On an imaginary scale of 0 to 100 percent (imagine a gauge) what is your inner receiving at this moment?
10. Notice if they are the same or different. Either way, it's time to bump them up as high as they will go in that moment. Any amount of increase is enormously beneficial!
11. Envision giving these two gauges to your heart area and awareness, from love. Imagine showing these two gauges to your body so that you can integrate this upgrade as a team.

Observe what it feels like in your body and senses to have this new experience in present time.
12. Repeat this again in a few days or a week.
13. Fill with golden suns of inner givingness, receiving, and enthusiasm for 100 percent permission.

Activity 2
Free Your Creative Energy by Asking Validating Questions

Verbal and nonverbal messages that make us believe we must fulfill unattainable perfection (that is never enough) keep us from stepping into the spacious flow of creative movement. Pushing that perfectionistic ideal away makes it stick more closely! Decide to accept your areas of supposed imperfections and reclaim your creative energy. In this activity, you will choose invalidating questions from a sample list and switch to validating questions to set your sights on manifesting your life's highest purposes. You can repeat this as many times as you like since practice makes perfect! Ha, now *there's* some old messaging! Actually, practice creates effort-free orchestration!

Directions
1. Sit in a chair with your feet on the floor. Give yourself three conscious breaths.
2. Thank your amazing body and say, "We are a conscious and creative team."
3. Greet yourself as the soul presence you are by validating your bright light and your power within. Say *Hello* to yourself! Quiet your analyzer by asking it to turn down the volume or intensity level to an optimized, balanced level for you in the present moment.
4. Be centered behind your eyes in your neutral awareness, in the present moment.

5. Ground yourself (Chapter 4, Activity 1). Set your energy in a high vibrational frequency, such as appreciation, joy, enthusiasm, humor, and/or playful curiosity, using the Golden Sun activity (Chapter 1, Activity 1).
6. Choose an area where you feel easily invalidated, or thrown off, even though you might intellectually tell yourself it's silly to be so impacted by that area. Validate, "Look at all those bookmarked pictures!" And remember you are not a picture or emotion; you are a bright, powerful presence!
7. Let your intuition highlight an invalidating question that is related to your chosen area and notice if this question is loudly barking or quietly lurking. Either way, it's generating a critical viewpoint somewhere in the back of your mind.
8. When you find the invalidating question showing up as a critical viewpoint, don't resist it, say *Hello*! It may even sound like someone you know. Decide to switch it out and replace it with 100 percent self-permission for love, abundance, compassion, and joy. Let that question or viewpoint be dissolved by the brightness of your awareness and by your inner laughter or compassion. Use the bubble-popping activity to clear thoughts, emotions, and/or pictures.
9. What question would better serve you in present time, with creating a new experience of your life and of your next creative steps from wholeness and unity?
10. Notice the list of examples of validating and invalidating questions below, to give you a few ideas, but don't limit yourself to that list.
11. Ask to be updated to present time with your new *what* question and say it out loud so you can hear it. Maybe this will make you laugh or smile.
12. Say *Hello* to your soul-body wholeness and unity, and then ask this question out loud again. Put it in writing where you can read it every day.

13. Give it 100 percent space to "be" in your beingness. Say *Hello* to your intuition, creativity, imagination, feelings, and intellect working collaboratively together as a soul-body team and observe what that's like for you.
14. Fill yourself with golden suns of self-love.

Sample list of invalidating questions:

- Am I good enough?
- Am I lovable enough?
- Am I accomplished enough?
- Am I busy enough?
- Am I smart enough?
- Am I responsible enough?
- Am I perfect enough?
- Am I physically attractive enough?

Sample list of validating questions:

- What creative and authentic approach will support the sharing of my gifts, skills, intuitive awareness, innate healing abilities, and communication?
- What qualities or actions will help restore my intuitive biome to harmony and well-being?
- What next steps will support me to apply or express my courage, neutrality, compassion, enthusiasm, love, or freedom?
- What next steps will engage my creative power as a soul-body team from wholeness and unity?
- What qualities, words, feelings, or actions nourish and cultivate my abundant creativity and creative expression?
- What qualities, words, feelings, or actions validate and support my intuitive knowing?
- What can I appreciate in this moment that shows me something I have not yet seen or recognized about what I can create or receive?

Activity 3
Creating Your Mock-Up Bubble

As creative director of your life, you can create a conscious mock-up of what you would like to experience or manifest. Many people create unconscious mock-ups, with varied results. This intuitive tool will help you to clearly envision, and then release unconscious energy as pictures (thoughts, emotions, opinions, outer directives, and self-doubts) that can show up as resistance energy dividing you from receiving what you are consciously setting your sights on.

When you wake up in the morning, you can create a simple mock-up for the way you'd like to experience and navigate the busy or complex day that lies ahead of you. This will allow for more inner support, improved qualities, clarity, and space to be aware, even when outer circumstances might stay the same. Quite often, outer circumstances will miraculously shift, saving you time and energy because it sets space for your approach or creates space for an orchestrated change of circumstances that are better all-around for everyone involved. This is one way that you can make and set space for your desired outcomes.

Your mock-up can also be a longer-term goal that you are working toward such as a business or creative project you are working on, a next step in your career or life, or a type of positive relationship that you would like to cultivate (with your child, community, partner, friend). It might also be an inner quality that you would like to experience more often in your daily life like inner trust, abundance, compassion, self-love, self-worth, or creativity.

Directions
1. Sit in a chair with your feet on the floor. Give yourself three conscious breaths.
2. Thank your amazing body by saying *Hello* to all the ways you are an embodied, harmonious team.
3. Greet yourself as the soul presence you are by validating your bright light and your power within. Say *Hello* to yourself! Quiet your analyzer by asking it to turn down the volume or intensity

level to an optimized, balanced level for you in the present moment.
4. Be centered behind your eyes in your neutral awareness, in the present moment.
5. Ground yourself (Chapter 4, Activity 1). Set your energy in a high vibrational frequency, such as appreciation, joy, enthusiasm, humor, and/or playful curiosity, using the Golden Sun activity (Chapter 1, Activity 1).
6. Give yourself 100 percent permission to imagine a giant bubble as big as you like that starts about four feet in front of you. Choose what you would like to manifest and experience. Imagine that you are adding positive, beneficial, supportive qualities in relation to your mock-up into this gigantic bubble.
7. Imagine this bubble has a cord attached to the bottom of it that can release energy down into the earth to be neutralized. After you have spent as much time as you like filling your bubble with positive, present-time qualities that will support your mock-up, imagine that any energy in resistance to this happening drains down the cord like water down a bathtub drain.
8. Once you have allowed any divisive unconscious energy to leave your bubble, what remains is the purest iteration of your manifestation mock-up. Give yourself 100 percent permission to have this manifest as you imagined it or in an even more aligned way for your highest benefit. Imagine your bubble is filled with an enormous golden sun full of infinite life force energy. Ask that your mock-up be blessed for the highest good to manifest with divine timing in spacious orchestration, then imagine cutting the cord and tying it off like a balloon.
9. Allow this bubble to be completely released to the universe so that you can fully receive the benefits of creative and intuitive orchestration.
10. Congratulate yourself, soul and body, for all you are: A loving, unified team, joyfully creating from wholeness.

Your Intuitive Toolbox Is Ready for Action

You now have an intuitive toolbox that empowers you to be the conscious director of your life. Intuitive awareness allows you to set your sights on new possibilities and graceful inner direction instead of chasing survival thinking's mad march into five different directions at the same time. Practicing your everyday intuition builds trust in your discernment and clarity, and helps you to continuously heal, grow, and expand. Laughter and humor lead you to a higher energy frequency, to experience having more fun and getting more done while being grounded in the present. All of this inner teamwork guides you into divine purposeful creation.

If you are saying *Hello* to a space that supports creating from your own energy or power, then you are on the right track. Consciously releasing bookmarked pictures changes your energy in an instant so that you can manage your whole space from unity. This helps you become aware of what you've been unconscious about, and recognize, explore, or discover what your true questions really are.

You shine your brightest when you are being yourself. Being yourself results from truly knowing yourself, valuing yourself, and trusting in yourself to imagine and see what lies beneath the surface. When you align being yourself with a form of expression, what results is authenticity and joy.

> ***Now, you can apply all your intuitive tools as a soul-body team and start living as the conscious creative director of your life! Celebrate!***

Acknowledgements

I send gratitude and love to all my students and clients, past and present. You inspired this book.

My deepest appreciation is to my amazing publishing team for believing in this book, and for expertly guiding it to the fullest expression of its potential with so much care: Michelle Vandepas, Tascha Yoder, Amy Delcambre, Laurie Knight, Erin Tackitt, and Mark Packard. Thank you to my beta readers for your insightful, enthusiastic, and supportive feedback exactly when I needed it: Sid Nair, Dr. Erin Sepic, Eleanor D'Aponte, Abby van den Berg, Ida Mitchell, Robin Jeffers, and Sue Mowrer Adamson. Thanks to Corrine Casanova for your exceptional support, and to Jen Mathews and Miranda Beverly-Whitmore for your kind writerly advice. Heartfelt appreciation to Raphaelle Tamura, and all my fellow SHAPESTERS everywhere! Thank you, Mary Bell Nyman. Love to Dr. Gayle P. Myers and the Vermont community. Love and gratitude to my parents, Jean and Doug, and my sister Sarah. Big love to my home team, Matt and Galadriel, for being who you are and sharing this wild adventure called life with me.

xo,
Gwyneth

About the Author

Gwyneth Flack loves guiding people to consciously integrate their intuitive awareness with their gifts, find their own answers, and experience joyful soul-body communication that supports their personal and professional purposes. She helps people awaken and amplify their intuition, inner laughter, and creativity to improve relationships, experience deeper insight, heal from past experiences, and become grounded while on the go in a nonstop world.

Gwyneth has been deeply aware of her intuitive and creative abilities since she was a child when she had a near-death experience that expanded her spiritual awareness. She completed advanced trainings in meditation, healing, and intuitive development, for the pure love of it! She cofounded and codirected a center for intuitive development which served the New England area and Canada for ten years. Since

2007, Gwyneth has given thousands of intuitive awareness-based classes and private sessions. Among her students are mental health and healthcare professionals, business entrepreneurs, professors, schoolteachers, artists, leaders, writers, parents, and teens.

As a member of Without Walls, an international community of advanced seers and healers from all backgrounds, she supported others in fulfilling their purposes, each with their own unique skill areas, to improve the conditions of the world. She has also collaborated behind the scenes with colleagues who bring intuitive tools to support children in urban underserved schools.

Gwyneth, born in New Zealand, moved to the United States as a child. She also lived in Asia where she taught, explored, and traveled widely and then in the UK where she earned her MA in creative writing. She now loves adventuring with her husband and teenage daughter, Galadriel. Gwyneth co-stewards a diverse forest ecosystem in Vermont with her husband, Matt, where they have an organic maple syrup production and retail business.

    Find her at gwynethflack.com.

For more great books from Empower Press
Visit Books.GracePointPublishing.com

If you enjoyed reading *Limitless*, and purchased it through an online retailer, please return to the site and write a review to help others find the book.